ARTIFICIAL INTELLIGENCE
Story & History

Safa Al Ameri

ISBN: 9798428339420

Cover design by: Simon Grange
Printed in the United States of America

2nd Edition

DEDICATION

I greatly appreciate the input and advice from Simon Grange, who, as the Editor, rode this wave with me and Alberto Chierici (author of The Ethics of AI) who inspired me to take on this project.

I thank my family for their encouragement having made this a pleasure and the team at Heriot Watt University in Dubai Computer Science; including Dr Abrar Ullah and Dr Ryad Soobhany, for their support and of course, living up to the series theme; providing me with *AI Insights*.

CONTENTS

FOREWORD

The AI Insights Series is both a reflection of the personal experience of the authors coming to live with AI, and the essence of understanding how we can augment our own intelligence by using such tools. The series 'deep dives' into specific areas with experts in each domain.

The first in the series by Safa Al Ameri demonstrates that with will and determination - great things are achievable. This foundation to the series aligns well as the books are intended to be both easily read and portable, so they may be carried with you to fill those gaps in the day.

As part of a community of AI specialists, we believe strongly in "explainable" AI, to demystify and help people with the awareness of how such tools will be part of our everyday lives.

Dr   Simon   Grange   (Ed.)

INTRODUCTION

You would have been scoffed at if you said "artificial intelligence" in a boardroom ten years ago. Most people would associate it with sentient, sci-fi machines like HAL from 2001: A Space Odyssey or Data from Star Trek. It is now one of the most popular buzzwords in business and industry. As companies position themselves to benefit from the ever-increasing quantity of data being produced and gathered, AI technology is a key lynchpin of much of today's digital transformation.

So, how did this change occur? Part of the reason for this is the Big Data revolution itself. The abundance of data has prompted increased research into how it can be processed, analysed, and acted upon. Because machines are far better suited to humans than this work, the emphasis was on teaching machines to do it as "smartly" as possible.

This increased interest in field research – in academia, industry, and the open-source community, which sits in the middle – has resulted in breakthroughs and advances that have the potential to generate enormous change. Artificial intelligence is being used in various areas, from healthcare to self-driving vehicles, to forecasting the result of court cases.

This book investigates the concept of artificial intelligence, its ethics, history, and importance. You will learn the idea of augmented intelligence, bio-inspired computing, its importance, and role in daily life. The book teaches you everything you need to know as a 'primer' about artificial intelligence and its future.

CHAPTER ONE

UNDERSTANDING ARTIFICIAL INTELLIGENCE (AI)

The term "artificial intelligence" elicits strong feelings. For one thing, there's our fascination with intelligence, which appears to give us humans a unique place among life forms. Questions such as "What is intelligence?" "How can intelligence be measured?" and "How does the brain work?" arise. All these questions are relevant when attempting to comprehend artificial intelligence. However, the central question for the engineer, particularly the computer scientist, is that of the intelligent machine that behaves like a person and exhibits intelligent behavior.

The attribute 'artificial' may arouse a wide range of associations. It instills fear of intelligent cyborgs, reminiscent of images from science fiction novels. It begs the question of whether we should try to understand, model, or even reconstruct our highest good, the soul.

With so many different *ad hoc* interpretations, it's difficult to define artificial intelligence (AI) simply and robustly. Nonetheless, I'd like to attempt to characterise the field of AI using examples and historical definitions. One of the pioneers of AI, John McCarthy, was the first to define the term artificial intelligence in 1955, roughly as follows: *The goal of AI is to develop machines that behave as if they were intelligent.*

To put this definition to the test, consider the following scenario. On a four by four-meter square enclosed surface, fifteen or so small robotic vehicles are moving. Various behavioural patterns can be observed. Some vehicles travel in small groups with little movement. Others move through the space peacefully and gracefully, avoiding any collisions. Others appear to be following a leader. Aggressive behaviour is also visible. Is the behaviour we're witnessing intelligent?

The robots are intelligent, according to McCarthy's definition. Valentin Braitenberg, a psychologist, demonstrated that very simple electrical circuits could produce this seemingly complex behaviour.

Braitenberg vehicles have two wheels, each of which is powered by its own electric motor. A light sensor on the front of the vehicle influences the speed of each motor. The more light hits the sensor, the faster the motor runs. Vehicle 1 in the left part of the figure moves away from a point light source according to its configuration. Vehicle 2, on the other hand, moves in the direction of the light source. Smaller changes can result in other behavior patterns, allowing us to achieve these very simple vehicles' impressive behaviour described above.

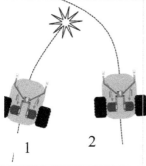

Figure 1: The Braitenberg vehicles have two wheels, each of which is powered by its own electric motor

Clearly, the above definition is insufficient because AI aims to solve difficult practical problems that are undoubtedly too difficult for the Braitenberg vehicle. According to the Encyclopedia Britannica, AI is *"the ability of digital computers or computer-controlled robots to solve problems that are normally associated with the higher intellectual processing capabilities of humans..."*

However, this definition has flaws. It would admit, for example, that a computer with a large memory that can save and retrieve a long text on demand demonstrates

intelligent capabilities because memorisation of long texts can certainly be considered a higher intellectual processing capability of humans, as can quick multiplication of two 20-digit numbers.

Then, by this definition, every computer is an AI system. Elaine Rich's definition elegantly solves this problem: *Artificial intelligence is the study of how to make computers do things that humans are currently better at.*

AI researchers have been doing this for the last 50 years, rich, terse, and concise. This definition will be current even in the year 2050. Digital computers' strong points are tasks such as executing many computations in a short amount of time. In this regard, they outperform humans by orders of magnitude. In many other areas, however, humans outperform machines. For example, a person entering an unfamiliar room will recognize the surroundings in fractions of a second and, if necessary, make decisions and plan actions in the same amount of time. This task is currently too difficult for autonomous robots. This is thus a task for AI, according to Rich's definition. In fact, research on autonomous robots is a hot topic in AI. On the other hand, chess computer construction has lost relevance, because they can already play at or above the level of grandmasters.

However, drawing the conclusion from Rich's definition that AI is only concerned with the pragmatic implementation of intelligent processes would be dangerous. Intelligent systems, according to Rich's definition, cannot be built without a thorough understanding of human reasoning and intelligent action in general, which is why neuroscience is so important in AI. This also demonstrates that the other definitions cited reflect important aspects of AI.

Adaptivity is a particular strength of human intelligence. We can adapt to different environmental conditions and change our behaviour because of learning. According to Rich's definition, machine learning is a central subfield of AI, because our learning ability is vastly superior to that of computers.

TYPES OF AI

Reactive Machines

A reactive machine adheres to the most fundamental AI principles and, as the name suggests, can only use its intelligence to perceive and react to the world in front of it. Because a reactive machine lacks memory, it cannot rely on past experiences to inform real-time decision-making.

Because reactive machines perceive the world directly, they can only perform a limited number of specialised tasks. However, deliberately limiting the worldview of a reactive machine is not a cost-cutting strategy; rather, it implies that this kind of AI will be more trustworthy and dependable and will respond consistently to the same stimuli.

Deep Blue, an example of a reactive machine, was created by IBM in the 1990s as a chess-playing supercomputer and defeated international grandmaster Gary Kasparov in a game. Deep Blue could only identify the pieces on a chess board and know how each moves according to the rules of chess, acknowledge each piece's current position, and determine what the most logical move would be at that time. The computer was not anticipating potential moves by its opponent or attempting to better position its pieces. Every turn was regarded as a separate reality, distinct from any previous movement.

Google's AlphaGo is another example of a reactive game-playing machine. AlphaGo is also incapable of predicting future moves instead it relies on its neural network to assess current game developments, giving it an advantage over Deep Blue in a more complex game. AlphaGo has also defeated world-class Go players, including champion Lee Sedol in 2016.

Though limited in scope and difficult to modify, reactive machine artificial intelligence can achieve a level of complexity and reliability when designed to perform repeatable tasks.

Limited Memory

When gathering information and weighing potential decisions, artificial intelligence with limited memory can store previous data and predictions — essentially looking into the past for clues on what may come next. Artificial intelligence with limited memory is more complex and offers more possibilities than reactive machines.

Memory problems: AI is created when a team continuously trains a model to analyse and use new data or when an AI environment is built to allow models to be automatically trained and renewed. Six steps must be taken when using limited memory AI in machine learning: Training data must be generated, a machine learning model must be developed, the model must be capable of making predictions, the model must be capable of receiving human or environmental feedback, that feedback must be recorded as data, and these steps must be repeated in a loop.

There are three main machine learning models for artificial intelligence with limited memory are:
- Reinforcement learning, which teaches itself to make better predictions through trial and error.
- Long Short-Term Memory (LSTM) uses previous data to predict the next item in a sequence. When making predictions, LTSMs prioritise recent information and

discount data from the past, though they still use it to draw conclusions.

- Evolutionary Generative Adversarial Networks (E-GAN) grow over time, exploring slightly modified paths based on previous experiences with each new decision. This model is always looking for a better path and uses simulations, statistics, or chance to predict outcomes throughout its evolutionary mutation cycle.

Theory of Mind

Theory of Mind is, well, theoretical. We don't currently have the technical and scientific capacity to reach this next level of artificial intelligence.

The theory is founded on the psychological assumption that other living creatures have thoughts and feelings that influence one's actions. This implies that AI machines will be able to comprehend how people, animals, and other machines feel and make choices via self-reflection and determination and will be able to utilise that knowledge to make their own judgments. To create a two-way connection between humans and artificial intelligence, machines would have to be able to understand and interpret the notion of "mind," the fluctuations of emotions in decision making, and a plethora of other psychological concepts in real-time.

Self-awareness

Once the Theory of Mind has been established in artificial intelligence, the final step will be for AI to become self-aware. This kind of artificial intelligence is conscious on a human level, aware of its existence in the environment and the presence and emotional condition of others. It would be able to deduce what others may need based on what they say to them and how they say it.

Self-awareness in artificial intelligence is dependent on both human researchers comprehending the premise of consciousness and then learning how to replicate it so that it can be built into machines.

Problem Solving and Brain Science

We can try to understand how the human brain works by researching intelligent systems and then modeling or simulating them on a computer. Many ideas and principles in the field of neural networks originate in brain science and the related field of neuroscience.

Taking a goal-oriented approach, starting with a problem, and finding the best solution, results in a very different approach. The method by which humans solve the problem is unimportant in this context. The method is secondary in this approach. The best intelligent solution to the problem comes first.

Rather than using a fixed method (such as predicate logic), AI's constant goal is to create intelligent agents capable of performing as many different tasks as possible. Because the tasks may be quite different, it is not surprising that the methods currently used in AI are frequently quite different. Like medicine, which encompasses a wide range of often life-saving diagnostic and therapeutic procedures, AI provides a diverse palette of effective solutions for many applications. There is no common approach for all AI application fields, just as there is no universal method for all medical applications; rather, there are numerous potential solutions for various daily issues, large and small.

Cognitive science is concerned with higher-level research into human thinking. This field, like brain science, provides many important ideas for practical AI. On the other hand, algorithms and implementations lead to additional important conclusions about how human reasoning works. As a result, these three disciplines benefit from a fruitful interdisciplinary exchange. However, the focus of this book is primarily on problem-oriented AI as a sub-discipline of computer science.

There are numerous philosophical questions that surround intelligence and artificial intelligence. Humans have consciousness, which means we can think about ourselves and even contemplate the fact that we can think about ourselves. How does consciousness emerge? Many philosophers and neurologists now believe that the mind and consciousness are inextricably linked to matter, specifically the brain. The question of whether machines can ever have a mind or consciousness may become relevant in the future.

CHAPTER TWO
THE HISTORY AND FUNCTION OF AI

Although AI as a term was first introduced in 1956, it has grown in prominence in recent years due to increasing data quantities, sophisticated algorithms, and improvements in computing power and storage. In the 1950s, early A.I. research focused on topics such as problem-solving and symbolic methods. The US Department of Defense got interested in this kind of work in the 1960s and started teaching computer systems to think like humans. The Defense Advanced Research Studies Agency (DARPA), for example, conducted street mapping projects in the 1970s. Before Siri, Alexa, or Cortana became household names, DARPA created intelligent personal assistants in 2003.

This pioneering work opened the path for today's automation and formal reasoning in computers, such as decision support systems and smart search systems, which may be built to improve and augment human skills. While Hollywood films and science fiction books portray AI as humanoid robots that take over the world, the present state of AI technology is neither scary nor smart. Rather, Artificial Intelligence has advanced to provide numerous specific benefits in every industry. Continue reading for examples of artificial intelligence in healthcare, retail, and other fields.

Why is AI so important?

The difference between AI and hardware-driven robotic automation is that the former does not depend on physical manipulation to complete its task, but rather uses data analysis. This means it can be used for tasks such as searching through large volumes of information or completing repetitively learned routines with minimal human intervention; in other words - artificial intelligence! Humans are still required to set up and ask the right questions for this type of automation.

AI augments existing items with intelligence. Intelligence is now available on any product you can think of. The AI will be integrated into existing items, but it's not sold as a separate application in most cases. Instead we're seeing this technology as an upgrade, added to already existing products, as Siri was for Apple devices with their latest update! Many homes and workplace advances, ranging from security intelligence to investment analysis, can be improved by combining automation, conversational platforms, bots, and smart devices with huge quantities of data.

AI adapts by allowing information to do the programming through progressive learning algorithms. Artificial intelligence (A.I.) finds structure and regularities in data, enabling the algorithm to become a classifier or predictor in the future. Consequently, just as an algorithm can train itself to play chess, one can also educate itself on what item to suggest next on the internet. And when new data is introduced, the models adjust. Back-propagation is an Artificial Intelligence technique that allows the model to adjust itself through training and additional data when the first answer is incorrect, each cycle reducing its error, *i.e.* learning.

AI uses neural networks with many hidden layers to analyze more through 'chaining' together differential equations and thus deeper neural network analysis of the data. It was nearly impossible to build a scam detection system with five 'hidden layers' of a neural network a few years ago. All of that has changed because of extraordinary computer power and vast amounts of data. With a huge quantity of data, deep learning algorithms can learn more about what they are analysing and become increasingly precise.

Deep neural networks, which were previously unthinkable, allow AI to achieve very high precision, being both specific and accurate. Here's an example: your interactions with Alexa,

Google Search, and Google Photos are all based on deep learning, and they continue to improve as we use them. Deep learning, image categorisation, and 'thing' recognition A.I. strategies can now be used in the medical field to detect cancer on MRIs with the same accuracy as highly trained radiologists.

AI makes the best use of data. When algorithms self-learn, the information itself may become copyrighted. The answers are in the data; all that is required is the application of Artificial Intelligence to extract them. Because the role of data is more important than ever before, it can provide a competitive advantage. If you have the best data in a competitive market, even if everyone else is using comparable strategies, you will win.

What are the drawbacks of utilising artificial intelligence?

There are a few potential drawbacks to utilising artificial intelligence. One is that AI systems can be biased if they are not trained properly. Another is that AI can be expensive to implement and maintain. Finally, some people worry about the possibility of artificial intelligence becoming smarter than humans and potentially pose a threat to our existence.

Each market will be altered by artificial intelligence, but we must first understand its limitations. A.I.'s concept constraint is that it learns from data. There is no other way for knowledge to be integrated. This means that any inaccuracies in the data will be reflected in the results. Any additional layers of prediction or analysis must be added individually.

Today's Artificial Intelligence systems are programmed to perform a specific task. The poker system is incapable of playing solitaire or chess. The system that detects scams cannot drive a car or provide legal advice. An Artificial Intelligence system that detects health care fraud is incapable of detecting tax or service warranty claims fraud.

In other words, these systems are highly specialized for 'narrow' fields, hence 'narrow AI'. They are oblivious to their surroundings and do not act like humans. Furthermore, self-learning systems are not self-contained systems. The imagined A.I. innovations seen in movies and television are still science fiction. However, computer systems that can sift through complex data to learn and perfect specific jobs are becoming more common. Beyond the limitations of performance, are the limitations of control.

I asked an AI the following question, what are the draw backs of Artificial Intelligence? To its answer: In computer science, artificial intelligence or AI is the simulation of intelligent behavior in computers. It is the science and engineering of making intelligent machines, especially intelligent computer programs.

According to a prominent researcher in the field, Max Tegmark (a MIT physics professor who has studied the origins of the universe and its many complexities), the first reason why we should fear the future of artificial intelligence is that it is within our ability to build artificial superintelligence. Artificial intelligence has the capacity to develop intelligence on a scale that's millions of times greater than the human mind's ability to do. Artificial super-intelligence could either be used as a tool to develop other technologies or create technological singularity wherein it separates from the human being and starts its own evolution. If left unchecked, this development could pose an existential threat to humanity.

Today, the most powerful forms of artificial intelligence are being used to make our lives easier, provide answers and improve the way we do things. However, there is a dark side to artificial intelligence as well, which we should be concerned about. There are a number of reasons to worry about the future of artificial intelligence.

Learning from mistakes is difficult for AI. This poses a danger because in the event of a major failure with an AI system, it may escalate out of control and lead to harmful consequences or even an apocalyptic scenario. If this happens, it may have devastating consequences for human civilisation as we know it today.

Another major problem associated with the development of AI is that it will lead to a major unemployment crisis soon, with 85% of jobs estimated to be affected over the next decade. Many people around the world are dependent on their jobs for their livelihood. Thus, if jobs start to get replaced by AI, it will be a disaster for many millions of people. On the other hand, some people believe that this problem can be solved by implementing a universal basic income for people as robots take over their jobs. Although this idea has merit, it is still far from reality given the current economic realities.

A third imagined scenario as to why we should be concerned about the rise of AI is the potential for the machines to take over the world and replace humans altogether. The argument goes that in the future, we will probably see the rise of humanoid robots that can learn from their mistakes just like human beings do. Thus, it won't be long before these machines start outsmarting us and becoming smarter than us. Once this happens, they will start to take over and enslave the human race like in the movie The Terminator.

In this scenario, we are basically destined to become slaves to the machines, and we will not be able to stop them from doing this. This is a terrifying prospect and one that we need to take seriously before it's too late. Therefore, there is no doubt that we should all be worried about the future implications of the rise of artificial intelligence. Fortunately, there are a number of steps that we can take to ensure that this doesn't become a problem in the future. These steps include developing alternative forms of energy, eliminating poverty and inequality in society, and educating our children from a young age so that they can develop the necessary skills to one day help contribute to the development of artificial intelligence. All these measures will go a long way towards ensuring that we remain in control of our own destiny in the future.

Nevertheless, there are also several steps that we can take to mitigate the possible negative consequences of the development of artificial intelligence. For example, we need to start developing ways to protect ourselves against the AI takeover by putting restrictions on the development of this technology. This can be done by imposing strict regulations on companies who are developing AI software to minimise the risk of a future 'robot uprising'.

Furthermore, it is our moral duty to protect humanity from the negative repercussions of the development of AI technology by doing everything that we can to ensure that these technologies are used for the good of mankind rather than for evil purposes. If we fail to do this, then we will eventually end up losing control of our own destiny and being controlled by our own creations.

HOW DOES ARTIFICIAL INTELLIGENCE WORK?

AI allows software to learn automatically from patterns or functions in the data by combining huge quantities of data with rapid, repeated processing and clever algorithms. A.I. is a broad discipline that includes many theories, methods, and technologies and the major subfields listed below: Machine learning automates the creation of analytical models. It employs techniques from neural networks, data science, operations research, and physics to uncover hidden data insights without explicitly being programmed as to where to look or what to conclude.

Most simply, artificial intelligence can be defined as a set of algorithms that allow machines to observe and learn from data, and then make predictions or decisions based on what they have learned. There are different types of AI algorithms, but some of the most common are:- Supervised learning algorithms: These algorithms learn from training data that has been labeled with the correct answers. For example, a supervised learning algorithm could be trained on a dataset of images that have been labeled as "dog" or "not dog." Once the algorithm has learned from this training data, it can then be given new images to classify.

Unsupervised learning algorithms: These algorithms learn from data that is not labeled. For example, an unsupervised learning algorithm could be given a dataset of images and asked to find patterns in the data. Algorithms are only one part of machine learning. Another important part is the model. The model is what makes predictions or decisions based on the data that the algorithms have learned from. There are different types of machine learning models, but some of the most common are:- Linear regression models: These models make predictions by finding the line of best fit for a dataset.

Logistic regression models: These models make predictions by finding the logistic function that best fits a dataset.

Neural networks: These models make predictions by using a series of interconnected nodes, like the way that neurons are interconnected in the brain.

Machine learning algorithms are constantly improving, and as they do, so does the accuracy of the predictions and decisions that they make. Therefore, artificial intelligence is such an important and rapidly growing field; because as machine learning algorithms get better, so does the artificial intelligence that we can create with them.

Cognitive computing is a field of artificial intelligence that seeks to provide computers with natural, human-like interactions. The aim of artificial intelligence (AI) and cognitive computing is for a machine to imitate human processes by interpreting pictures and voices and then reacting logically.

The cognitive computing market was valued at USD 4.03 Billion in 2016 and is expected to reach a market size of USD 19.06 Billion by 2023, at a CAGR of 28.6% during the forecast period. Cognitive computing systems have been developed with an aim to address the complexity of big data and provide insights that can help humans make better decisions. These systems are developed on the basis of cognitive architectures, which are a set of integrated technologies that work together to provide a complete cognitive system. The cognitive computing market is expected to grow owing to the increasing demand for AI-based applications, such as chatbots and digital assistants.

The major players in the cognitive computing market include IBM Corporation (US), Google LLC (US), Microsoft Corporation (US), AWS (US), Infosys Limited (India), Wipro Limited (India), Numenta, Inc. (US), IPsoft, Inc. (US), Rainbird Technologies, Inc. (US), Premonition AI, Inc. (US), and Freenome, Inc. (US). The cognitive computing market is expected to grow at a CAGR of 62.9% from 2018 to 2025 to reach USD 19.5 Billion by 2025.

To identify what's in an image or video, computer vision uses pattern recognition and deep learning. When devices can process, examine, and understand images, they can capture and translate images or videos in real-time.

Natural language processing refers to computers' ability to analyse, comprehend, and produce human language, including speech. Natural language interaction is the next stage of NLP, allowing people to communicate with computers using everyday language to perform tasks. Furthermore, certain technologies enable and support AI: Visual processing systems are critical to AI because they provide the high computing power needed for iterative processing. Training neural networks necessitate massive amounts of data as well as massive amounts of computing power.

The Internet of Things (IoT) produces enormous quantities of data from linked devices, the overwhelming majority of which is never examined. We will be able to use AI more effectively if we can automate models. To evaluate more data at various levels and at a quicker pace, advanced algorithms are being created and integrated into new ways. This intelligent processing is critical for detecting and forecasting rare events, comprehending complex systems, and optimising unique situations.

APIs, or application programming interfaces, are portable code packages that enable the addition of A.I. functionality to existing items and software application packages. They can enhance home security systems with image recognition capabilities and Q&A capabilities that describe information, generate captions and headings, or highlight fascinating patterns and insights in data.

In conclusion, the goal of AI is to provide software applications that can reason on input and clarify on output. Artificial intelligence will provide human-like interactions with software and decision support for specific jobs, but it is not a replacement for people and will not be anytime soon.

CHAPTER THREE
ETHICS OF AI

This chapter provides a thorough overview of the major ethical issues concerning the impact of Artificial Intelligence (AI) on human society. AI has had a rapid and significant impact on human society and how we interact with one another in many areas of human life. It will do so in the future. AI has presented significant ethical and sociopolitical challenges along the way, necessitating a thorough philosophical and ethical analysis. Its social impact should be investigated to avoid any negative consequences. AI systems are becoming increasingly autonomous, rational, and intelligent. This extensive development raises a slew of issues. Other problems include their moral and legal status (including moral and legal rights), possible moral agency and questions about their potential personality and even dignity.

As artificial intelligence (AI) continues to develop and become more sophisticated, it is increasingly important to consider the ethical implications of its use. AI has the potential to transform our lives in many positive ways, but it also poses significant risks if not used responsibly. There are several ethical concerns that need to be considered when developing and using AI, such as the impact of AI on privacy, the potential for bias in AI decision-making, and the risk of AI being used for harmful purposes.

The impact of AI on privacy: As AI gets better at understanding and predicting human behavior, there is a risk that it could be used to violate our privacy. For example, when an AI system is used to monitor our online activity or track our location, it is used to build up a detailed profile of our personal preferences and habits. This information could then be used for marketing purposes or sold to third parties without our knowledge or consent.

The impact of AI on safety: AI systems are increasingly being used in critical applications such as self-driving cars and medical diagnosis. These uses are not intentional 'killer robots'. If however, these systems are not designed and tested properly, there is a risk that they could malfunction in ways that could endanger human life.

The impact of AI on employment: As mentioned above, many jobs are at risk from automated by AI systems in the future. This could lead to large-scale unemployment and social unrest. However, it will create other jobs that do not exist now. According to Bernard Marr, an international bestselling author, futurist and technology adviser to governments and companies proposes the 'flip side' to change; 85 percent of the jobs that humans will do in 2030 don't exist yet!

The impact of decision making of AI: As AI systems become more intelligent, they will increasingly be able to make decisions that have ethical implications. For example, an autonomous car might have to choose between crashing into a wall and killing its passengers or swerving into oncoming traffic and killing other people. These are the kinds of decisions that humans currently make, but AI systems will soon be making them autonomously. However, based on three different eras, it is customary to categorise the problems as being of the greatest significance in terms of AI and its connection to human society:

(1) **H1:** (from the 2020s onwards): autonomous systems (transportation, weapons), machine bias in law, privacy and surveillance, the black box problem, and AI decision-making.

(2) **H2:** (from the 2030s onwards): AI governance, confirming

the moral and legal status of intelligent machines (artificial moral agents), human-machine interaction, and mass automation.

(3) **H3**: (from the 2040s onwards): technological singularity, widespread unemployment, and space Colonisation.

THE RELEVANCE OF AI FOR ETHICS

Given the increasing human-machine interaction, this section discusses why AI is critical for our systems of ethics and morality. Systems of ethics and morality are built around human beings. Yet as technology continues to evolve, it is important that we update our values for the future - or else risk losing what makes us human.

As we saw in Chapter 1, AI can imply a wide variety of things and can be defined in several ways. When Alan Turing presented the so-called Turing test (which he termed an "imitation game") in his famous 1950 article on whether computers can think, the phrase "artificial intelligence" had not yet been created. Turing pondered whether machines could think and suggested that the issue be replaced with whether it would be feasible to create machines that could successfully mimic humans to the point that people would be unable to distinguish whether a written message came from a computer or a person.

The aim of many computer scientists and engineers in the early twenty-first century was to create a reliable AI system that resembled human intellect in every aspect except its machine origin. For several decades, people have been debating whether this is even possible. The so-called 'The Chinese room argument', proposed by prominent American philosopher John Searle (1980), contends that strong or general AI (AGI) — that is, building AI systems capable of dealing with a wide range of complex tasks requiring human-like intelligence — is in principle impossible. As a result, he sparked a long-running general debate about the possibility of AGI. Current narrowly focused AI systems (*i.e.*, weak AI) can only solve one specific task, such as chess or the Chinese game of Go, described above. In contrast to the ability to compute, Searle's general thesis was that no matter how complex and sophisticated a machine is, it will still lack 'consciousness' or 'mind,' which is a prerequisite for the ability to understand.

Figure 2: The Chinese Room Argument in Artificial Intelligence
(Karbhari, 2020)

John Searle's argument has been scrutinized considering functionalism and computationalism's counterclaims. It is widely held that intelligence does not require a specific substratum, such as carbon-based beings, and that it can evolve in silicon-based environments if the system is complex enough. Functionalists claim that intelligence can only evolve in systems with a specific substrate, such as carbon-based beings. However, computationalists argue against this idea by saying it is possible for an intelligent system to exist without having any particular type of Being's qualities at all!

Many researchers working on AI development in the early years of the twenty-first century associated AI primarily with various forms of so-called machine learning—that is, technologies that identify patterns in data. Simpler forms of such systems are said to engage in "supervised learning," which still requires significant human input and supervision, but the goal of many researchers, perhaps most notably Yann Le Cun, has been to develop "self-supervised learning" systems. Supervised, Semi-Supervised, Unsupervised, and Self-Supervised Learning are the four core regimes in the field of machine learning. Some researchers have recently begun to discuss AI in a way that appears to equate the concept with machine learning. However, in this book, the term "AI" is used in a broader sense that includes but is not limited to machine learning technologies.

AI AND ITS RECENT ETHICAL IMPORTANCE

In outstanding introductions by Vincent Müller (2020), Mark Coeckelbergh (2020), Janina Loh (2019), Catrin Misselhorn (2018), and David Gunkel (2018), the main ethical problems that AI presents to human society are clearly outlined (2012). Regardless of how AGI is defined, autonomous AI systems already raise significant ethical concerns, such as machine bias in law, hiring decisions made by smart algorithms, racist and sexist chatbots, and non-gender-neutral language translations. The idea of a machine 'imitating' human intelligence—a popular definition of AI—raises worries about deception, particularly if the AI is integrated into robots that appear or behave like people. Furthermore, Rosalind Picard correctly asserts that *"the greater the freedom of a machine, the more it will require moral standards."* This supports the claim that all interactions between AI systems and humans, such as in the context of autonomous transportation, must include an ethical component.

One of the primary research goals in the field of machine ethics is to implement ethics within a machine. As evidenced by the excellent performance of many systems, more and more responsibility has been shifted from humans to autonomous AI systems, which can work much faster than humans without taking breaks and without the need for constant supervision (once they have successfully passed the debugging phase).

It has been suggested that the implementation of strong moral standards in AI systems may be critical to humanity's future survival, given the possibility that these systems will eventually match or surpass human capabilities. Vernon Vinge coined the term *"technological singularity"* in 1983 to describe this point in time. Famous playwright Karl Apek (1920), renowned astrophysicist Stephen Hawking, and influential philosopher Nick Bostrom (2016, 2018) have warned of the dangers of technological singularity if intelligent machines turn against their creators, humans. As a result, according to Nick Bostrom, it is critical to create friendly AI.

To summarise, the implementation of ethics is critical for AI systems for various reasons, including providing safety guidelines that can prevent existential risks for humanity, resolving bias issues, building friendly AI systems that will adopt our ethical standards, and assisting humanity in flourishing.

THE CONTEXT OF ARTIFICIAL INTELLIGENCE AND ETHICS

In the context of AI and ethics, the following debates are critical for business, research, or academics prospective. They are not the only significant arguments in the area, but they provide a fair overview of topics that will most likely remain relevant for decades.

Ethics of Machines

According to Susan Anderson, a pioneer in machine ethics, the goal of machine ethics is to create a machine that follows an ideal ethical principle or set of principles in guiding its behaviour; in other words, it is guided by this principle, or these principles, in making decisions about possible courses of action. To put it another way, this entails "adding an ethical dimension" to the machine.

Furthermore, the study of machine ethics investigates the moral status of intelligent machines and asks whether they should be granted moral and legal rights. Machine ethics is an interdisciplinary sub-discipline of applied ethics, which is itself a sub-discipline of technology ethics. Robot ethics, which is concerned with how humans design, construct and use robots, and computer ethics, which is concerned with commercial behaviour involving computers and information, are also sub-disciplines of technology ethics (for example, data security, privacy issues).

Isaac Asimov, the famed science fiction writer, presented his Three Laws of Robotics in 'Runaround', establishing the first ethical code for AI systems. In 'Robots and Empire', a fourth law, dubbed the Zeroth Law of Robotics, was added to these three.

0. A robot may not harm humanity, or, by inaction, allow humanity to come to harm.
1. A robot may not injure a human being, or, through inaction, allow a human being to come to harm.
2. A robot must obey the orders given it by human beings except where such orders.
3. A robot must protect its own existence so long as such protection does not conflict with the First or Second Laws.

For many decades, Asimov's four laws have played a significant role in machine ethics and have been widely debated by experts. According to popular belief, the four laws are important but insufficient to address all the complexities associated with moral machines. This appears to be a fair assessment, as Asimov never claimed that his laws could handle all problems. If that were true, Asimov might not have written his fascinating stories about problems caused in part by the four laws.

Anyone who codes, will appreciate 'exception handling'. Several approaches to implementing ethics within machines were proposed in the early years of the twenty-first century to provide AI systems with ethical principles that machines could use in making moral decisions (Gordon 2020a). There are at least three approaches to consider: bottom-up, top-down, and mixed, or how I like to call it, hybrid. Each type is represented by an example below.

I. Bottom-up Methodologies: Casuistry

The system developed by Guarini (2006) is an example of a bottom-up approach. It employs a neural network to make ethical decisions based on a learning process in which the neural network is presented with correct answers to ethical issues. Following the initial learning process, the system is expected to solve new ethical issues on its own. On the other hand, Guarini's method has problems with case categorization due to a lack of sufficient reflection and accurate depiction of the circumstance. Guarini acknowledges that casuistry is inadequate for machine ethics by itself.

II. Top-down Approaches: The Moral DM Method

Dehghani *et al.* (2011) developed a system that combines two major ethical theories, utilitarianism and deontology, and analogical reasoning. When 'sacred values' are involved, the system changes to a deontological mode and becomes less sensitive to the utility of acts and consequences, *i.e.,* when the system shifts to a deontological mode it becomes less sensitive to the usefulness of actions and consequences, such as the real-world productivity of AI. Dehghani *et al.* evaluate the system against psychological studies of how most human beings

28

decide specific cases to align it with human moral decisions.

The Moral DM method is especially successful because it honors and effectively integrates the two main ethical systems (deontology and utilitarianism). However, their added approach of utilising empirical studies to mimic human moral choices by only selecting those who agree with the majority view right is misleading and severely flawed. Instead of being regarded as a model for normative ethics, their system should be viewed as a model for a descriptive study of ethical behaviour.

III. Hybrid Approaches: A Combination of Approaches

The hybrid model of human cognition combines a top-down component (theory-driven reasoning) and a bottom-up component (shaped by evolution and learning) that are thought to be the foundations of both moral reasoning and decision-making. The outcome so far is LIDA, an AGI program that provides a complete conceptual and computational model that represents a significant part of human cognition. The hybrid model of moral reasoning seeks to recreate human decision-making by employing a complex combination of top-down and bottom-up approaches, eventually leading to a descriptive but not normative model of ethics. Furthermore, its somewhat idiosyncratic understanding of both moral philosophy approaches does not correspond to how moral philosophers understand and apply them in normative ethics.

The Wallach *et al.* model is not necessarily inaccurate in terms of empirically moral decision-making, but their approach is descriptive rather than normative. As a result, their empirical model does not address the normative issue of how moral machines should behave. Descriptive ethics and normative ethics are distinct concepts. The former describes how humans make moral decisions, while the latter addresses how we should act.

IV. Systems with Autonomy

The proposals for a machine ethics system are increasingly being discussed in relation to autonomous systems whose operation poses a risk to human life. The two most frequently discussed examples—which are sometimes discussed together, contrasted, and compared with one another—are autonomous vehicles (also known as self-driving cars) and autonomous weapons systems (also known as 'killer robots').

Some authors believe that self-driving weapons could be a viable replacement for human soldiers. For example, Arkin (2009, 2010) contends that having machines fight our wars instead of human soldiers could reduce war crimes if the machines were outfitted with an 'ethical governor' system that consistently followed the rules of war and engagement. Others, on the other hand, are concerned about the widespread availability of AI-driven autonomous weapons systems, either because they believe such systems will tempt people to go to war more frequently or because they are skeptical of the possibility of an AI system that can interpret and apply the ethical and legal principles of war. There is also concern that 'killer robots' could be hacked.

Similarly, while acknowledging the potential benefits of self-driving cars, such as increased traffic safety, reducing the 1.2 million needless deaths per year, more efficient fuel use, and better-coordinated traffic; many authors have also mentioned the potential for accidents. The fundamental concept is that self-driving cars should be equipped with 'ethical settings,' which would help determine how they should behave in accident situations affecting people's lives and safety. This is another real-world application of machine ethics with which humanity must immediately deal with.

Concerns about self-driving cars being involved in fatal accidents for which the AI system may not have been adequately prepared have already been realised, sadly, as some people have died in such accidents. The first death while riding in an autonomous vehicle occurred in May 2016, when a Tesla Model S car crashed in 'autopilot' mode. In March 2018, the first pedestrian was killed by an Uber self-driving vehicle in an experiment. In the latter instance, the car's AI system had trouble identifying the item that suddenly emerged in its path, which was part of the problem. It classified the victim as 'unknown' at first, then as a 'vehicle,' and finally as a 'bicycle' because the pedestrian was crossing the road whilst pushing a bicycle. The system decided to apply the brakes just moments before the crash, but it was too late. Whether or not the car's AI system works properly can thus be a matter of life and death.

Philosophers debating such cases may propose that it may swerve to one side even if the car cannot halt in time. But what if there were five people on the only side of the road where the car could swerve? What if there were five persons on the road, one of them was on the curb, where the car could swerve? These situations are analogous to the well-known 'trolley dilemma,' in which a decision must be made between killing one person and saving five, with the question of whether that action is acceptable under what conditions. The ethics of self-driving vehicle accidents, on the one hand, and the philosophy of the trolley issue, on the other, have been discussed in many publications. No one has the absolute answer.

One issue that ethicists debating autonomous systems have discussed is what ethical standards should guide their decision-making in circumstances when human beings may be harmed. A related question is whether for autonomous machines it is ever acceptable to kill or harm humans, particularly if they do so in accordance with certain principles that have been programmed into or otherwise made a part of the machines. In this case, a distinction is made between deaths caused by self-driving cars, which are widely regarded as a deeply regrettable but unavoidable side effect of their use, still safer than cars driven by humans, the current alternative; and killing by autonomous weapons systems, which some always consider morally unacceptable. Many AI ethicists, including Noel Sharkey and Peter Asaro, have even launched a campaign to 'stop killer robots.'

One of the campaign's arguments for banning autonomous weapons systems is that what they call "meaningful human control" must be preserved. This idea is also brought up in relation to self-driving cars. Many authors have expressed concern about the risk of creating 'responsibility gaps,' or cases in which it is unclear who should be held accountable for the harm caused by an autonomous AI system's decision. The key challenge here is to develop a way of understanding moral responsibility in the context of autonomous systems that allows us to secure such systems' benefits while appropriately attributing responsibility for any negative consequences. If a machine causes harm, the humans involved in the machine's action may try to avoid responsibility; indeed, in some cases, blaming people for what a machine has done may appear unfair. Of course, if an autonomous system produces a good result for which some humans, if any, claim credit, the outcome may be equally ambiguous. People may be more willing to accept responsibility for positive outcomes produced by autonomous systems than for negative ones. However, in both cases, there may be a lack of accountability. Consequently, philosophers must devise a theory for assigning blame for the results generated by functionally independent AI systems, whether positive or negative (Nyholm 2018a; Dignum 2019; Danaher 2019a; Tigard 2020a).

Machine Bias

Because of the supposed 'neutrality' of machines, many people believe that the use of smart technologies will eliminate human bias. However, we have discovered that machines can maintain and even substantiate human biases against women, different ethnicities, the elderly, people with medical impairments, and other groups. As a result, one of the most pressing questions in machine learning is how to avoid machine bias. The idea of using AI systems to assist human decision-making is, in general, a great goal given AI's *"increased efficiency, accuracy, scale, and speed in making decisions and finding the best answers"* (World Economic Forum 2018: 6). On the other hand, machine bias can undermine this seemingly positive situation in a variety of ways. The following are some notable examples of machine bias:

1.   Gender bias in hiring.
2.   Racial bias, in which certain racial groups are only offered certain types of jobs.
3.   Racial bias in decisions on loan applicants' creditworthiness.
4.   Racial bias in parole decisions.
5.   Racial bias in predicting criminal activity in urban areas.
6.   Sexual bias in determining a person's sexual orientation.
7.   Racial bias in facial recognition systems that prefer lighter skin tones or a certain racial group.
8.   Racial and social bias in using a person's residence's geographic location as a proxy for ethnicity or socioeconomic status.

At least three variables contribute to machine bias:
(1) data bias
(2) computational/algorithmic bias
(3) result bias (Springer *et al.* 2018: 451)

First, a machine learning system trained on data with implicit or explicit imbalances reinforces the data distortion in future decision-making, making bias systemic.

Second, a program may suffer from algorithmic bias due to the developer's implicit or explicit biases. A program's design is dependent on the developer's understanding of the normative and non-normative values of others, including the users and stakeholders who will be affected by it (Dobbe *et al.*, 2018).

Third, outcome bias may be based on the use of historical records, for example, to predict criminal activity in specific urban areas; the system may allocate more police to a specific area, resulting in an increase in reported cases that would have gone unnoticed previously. This logic would support the AI system's decision to allocate police to this area, even though other urban areas may have similar or even higher numbers of crimes, with more of them going unreported due to a lack of policing (O'Neil 2016).

Most AI researchers, programmers, developers, and technology scholars believe that we will never be able to design a completely unbiased system. As a result, the emphasis is on reducing machine bias and minimising its negative effects on humans. Nonetheless, several questions remain. What kinds of bias cannot be filtered out, and when should we be content with the remaining bias? What does it mean for a person in court to be subject to both human and machine bias, with both types of injustice potentially influencing the person's sentence? Is one type of bias insufficient? Shouldn't the goal be to eliminate human bias rather than to introduce a new one?

The Opacity Problem

AI systems are used to make a wide range of decisions that significantly impact people's lives. AI can be used to decide who gets a loan, who gets into a university, who gets an advertised job, who is likely to re-offend, and so on. We must understand the underlying reasons for these decisions because they have such a large impact on people. To put it another way, AI and its decision-making must be explicable. Indeed, many authors discussing the ethics of AI propose explainability (also known as explicability) as a fundamental ethical criterion for the acceptability of AI decision-making, among other things (Floridi *et al.*, 2018). However, many decisions made by an autonomous AI system are difficult to explain to humans. This became known as the opacity problem.

Depending on the relevant factors, the opacity of AI decision-making can be of various types. Some AI decisions are opaque to those affected by them because the algorithms underlying the decisions, while simple to understand, are protected trade secrets that the companies employing them do not want to share with anyone outside the company. Another reason for AI opacity is that most people lack the technical expertise required to understand how an AI-based system works, even if the technology in question is not inherently opaque. Even experts cannot understand the decision-making processes used by some forms of AI. This is known as the 'black box' problem.

Individually, it can appear to be an affront to a person's dignity and autonomy when machines make decisions about important aspects of their lives, especially if it is unclear — or perhaps impossible to know — why machines made these decisions. On a societal level, the growing prominence of algorithmic decision-making could endanger our democratic processes. 'We may have developed a dominant technology in need of a guiding philosophy,' remarked former US Secretary of State Henry Kissinger (Kissinger 2018; cited in Müller 2020). Commenting on this idea, John Danaher expresses concern that people will be led to act in superstitious and irrational ways, like those in the past who believed they could influence natural phenomena through rain dances or similar ritual behaviour. Danaher refers to this as the "threat of algocracy" — that is, rule by algorithms that we do not understand but must obey.

Is AI opacity, however, always, and necessarily a problem? If an AI system distinguishes accurately between a picture of a dog and a wolf because the latter has snow in the background of the picture, does this unexplained use of context matter? Is it equally problematic in all situations? Should there be an absolute requirement that AI be explainable in all cases?

Scott Robbins (2019) has made some interesting and noteworthy counterarguments to this idea. Robbins contends, that a strict requirement for explicability may prevent us from reaping all of AI's potential benefits. For example, if an AI system could consistently detect or forecast cancer in a manner that humans couldn't explain or comprehend, the benefit of knowing would exceed any worries about not understanding how the AI system came to this decision. In general, there are two types of contexts: those in which the procedure behind a decision is important in and of itself, and those in which only the quality of the outcome is important.

Another promising approach to the problem of opacity is to try to develop alternative modes of explaining AI decisions that consider their opacity while still providing some form of explanation that people can act on. Sandra Wachter, Brent Mittelstadt, and Chris Russell (2019) proposed the concept of a "counterfactual explanation" for such decisions, with the goal of providing practical guidance for people who want to respond rationally to AI decisions they don't understand. "Counterfactual explanations don't try to explain how [AI] choices are made inside," they claim. Rather, they reveal which external factors might be changed to obtain the desired result.' Such an external, counterfactual explanation for AI decisions could be a promising alternative in cases where AI decision-making is highly valuable but operates on an internal logic that is opaque to most or all people.

Machine Consciousness

Some researchers believe that as machines become more sophisticated and intelligent, they may eventually become spontaneously conscious as well (compare Russell 2019). This would be a perplexing but potentially significant side effect of advanced AI development from an ethical standpoint. Some people are attempting to create machines with artificial consciousness on purpose. Kunihiro Asada, a successful engineer, set the goal of creating a robot that can feel pleasure and pain on the premise that such a robot could engage in the kind of pre-linguistic learning that a human baby could do before learning to speak. Another example is Sophia, the robot, whose creators at Hanson Robotics say they want to create a "super-intelligent benevolent being" that will eventually become a "conscious, living machine."

Others, such as Joanna Bryson, argue that some machines may already have some form of consciousness depending on how consciousness is defined. According to Bryson, if consciousness is defined as internal states and the capacity to report these states to other agents, certain machines may already fulfill these requirements (Bryson 2012). Furthermore, Ada Elamrani-Raoult and Roman Yampolskiy (2018) identified up to twenty-one different possible tests of machine consciousness.

Similar arguments may be made regarding whether machines can think. Machines may have minds if mind is defined, at least in part, as the internal processing of external inputs that produce apparently intelligent reactions to that environment (Nyholm 2020: 145–46). Of course, even if robots have minds or awareness somehow, they are not necessarily the same as human minds. After all, the specific consciousness and subjectivity of any being will be determined by the types of 'hardware' (such as brains, sense organs, and nervous systems) that being possesses.

Whether we believe some AI machines are already conscious or that they could (by accident or design) become conscious, this is a major source of ethical debate. According to Thomas Metzinger (2013), as a fundamental principle of AI ethics, society should prohibit the creation of machines capable of suffering. His argument is straightforward: suffering is bad, causing suffering is immoral, and thus creating machines that suffer would be immoral. Similarly, Joanna Bryson contends that, while it is possible to create machines with significant moral status, it is best to avoid doing so; in her opinion, we are morally obligated not to create machines with which we would have obligations (Bryson 2010, 2019). Again, it may all depend on how we define consciousness. As a result, Eric Schwitzgebel and Mara Garza (2015: 114–15) write, *"If society continues on the path toward more sophisticated artificial intelligence, developing a good theory of consciousness is a moral imperative."*

Nicholas Agar (2019) offers another interesting perspective, arguing that if there are reasons both for and against the idea that some advanced machines have brains and awareness, we should err on the side of caution and continue on the premise that machines do. On that basis, we should abstain from any actions that might put them in harm's way. In contrast, John Danaher (2020) claims that we can never be certain whether a machine has the conscious experience, but that this uncertainty is irrelevant; if a machine behaves similarly to how conscious beings with moral status behave, this is enough moral reason, according to Danaher's 'ethical behaviourism,' to treat the machine with the same moral considerations as we would treat a conscious being. The standard approach considers whether machines have conscious minds and how this answer should influence the question of whether machines should be granted moral status.

CHAPTER FOUR
THE MORAL STATUS OF ARTIFICIAL INTELLIGENT MACHINES

Historically, the concept of moral status has been crucial in ethics and moral philosophy because entities with a moral status are considered members of the moral community and are entitled to moral protection. Because not all members of a moral community have the same moral status, their claims to moral protection differ. Dogs and cats, for example, are members of our moral community, but they do not have the same moral standing as adult human beings. If a being has moral status, it also has moral (and legal) rights. The twentieth century saw an increase in recognition of the rights of ethnic minorities, women, and certain communities and animal and environmental rights, usually consequent upon exposing their abuse. When artificial intelligent machines become available, this expanding moral circle may expand even further (as advocated by the robot rights movement).

The concept of personhood (whatever that means) has become relevant in determining whether an entity has full moral status and, if so, whether it should enjoy the full set of moral rights. Frances Kamm (2007: 229) provides a prominent definition of moral status:

So, within the class of entities that count, we see that there are those entities that could give us reason to act and for their own sake. This, I believe, is what people have in mind when they attribute moral status to an entity. As a result, from now on, I will distinguish between an entity counting morally in its own right and having moral status. I will say that an entity has moral status when it can give us reasons to do things like not destroy it or help it and for its own sake.

According to Kamm, things can be done for X's sake if X is

conscious and capable of feeling pain. Humans and most animals are typically included in this definition, whereas non-living parts of nature are primarily excluded due to their lack of consciousness and inability to feel pain. However, there are compelling reasons to broaden one's moral reasoning and decision-making to include the environment as well (Stone 1972, 2010; Atapattu 2015). Because of its unique form and high aesthetic value, the Grand Canyon, for example, could be morally considered in human decision-making despite its lack of personhood and thus moral status. Furthermore, some experts have treated sentient animals such as great apes and elephants as if they were humans, even though they are not.

Furthermore, we can raise the important question of whether (a) current social robots or (b) artificial intelligent machines, once created, may have moral status, and be entitled to moral rights comparable to human moral status and rights. The three main approaches presented below provide a brief overview of the discussion.

i. The Autonomy Strategy

Kant and his followers place a high value on the concept of autonomy in terms of moral standing and rights. A moral person is one who is rational and self-aware. Against this backdrop, it has been proposed that once artificial intelligent machines reach a certain level of autonomy in making moral decisions, they may be able to be assigned personhood. As machines become more autonomous, it appears that it will only be a matter of time before they reach this moral threshold. A Kantian line of argument in favour of granting moral status to machines based on autonomy might be as follows:

1.   Rational agents can choose whether to act (or not act) in accordance with moral demands.
    - The ability to make decisions and determine what is good is priceless.

- The ability to make such decisions confers absolute value on rational people.

2. A rational agent can act autonomously, including acting in accordance with moral principles.

- Insofar as they act autonomously, rational agents have dignity.
- Individuals are morally responsible when they act autonomously.

3. Such a being, *i.e.,* a rational agent, possesses moral personhood.

It could be argued that machines, no matter how autonomous and rational, are not human beings and thus do not have moral status and the rights that go with it under a Kantian framework. However, this objection is deceptive because Kant explicitly states in his Groundwork (2009) that humans should be considered moral agents not because they are humans but because they are autonomous agents. Kant's opponents have criticised him for his logocentrism, even though this claim has helped him avoid the more serious objection of speciesism—the belief that a particular species is morally superior solely because of empirical features of the species itself (in the case of human beings, the particular DNA). This has been widely regarded as the species-level equivalent of racism.

ii. The Approach Based on Indirect Duties

Kant's analysis of our behaviour toward animals serves as the foundation for the indirect duties approach. Kant argues in his Lectures on Ethics (1980: 239–41) that, while humans do not have direct duties to animals (because they are not persons), they do have indirect duties to them. The underlying reason is that if humans develop bad habits by mistreating and abusing animals as they see fit, they may begin to treat their fellow humans poorly. In other words, animal cruelty may have a negative, brutalising effect on human character.

Kate Darling (2016) used Kantian logic to demonstrate that even current social robots should be entitled to moral and legal protection. She contends that lifelike beings, such as robots that interact with humans, should be protected when society cares deeply enough about them, even if they do not have a right to life. Darling makes two arguments for why social robots should be treated in this manner. Her first argument is that people who witness robot abuse and mistreatment cases may become 'traumatised' and 'desensitised.' Second, she claims that abusing robots can negatively impact the abuser's character, leading her to treat other humans poorly as well.

Indeed, the indirect duties approach may best protect current social robots, but the idea that the same arguments should also be applied to future robots of greater sophistication that match or supersede human capabilities is troubling. Normally, one would expect these future robots, unlike Darling's social robots of today, to be more than just moral patients but also proper moral agents. Furthermore, the belief that one should protect lifelike beings "when society cares deeply enough" (2016: 230) about them opens the door to social exclusion based solely on people's refusal to accept them as members of the moral community. Morally, this is unacceptably bad. The following strategy attempts to deal with this situation.

iii. The Relational Method

The pioneers of the relational approach to moral status, Mark Coeckelbergh (2014) and David Gunkel (2012), believe that robots have moral status based on their social relationship with humans. In other words, moral status or personhood emerges from social interactions between different entities, such as humans and robots, rather than from criteria inherent in the being, such as sentience and consciousness. The general concept underlying this approach is highlighted in the following key passage:

We may wonder whether robots will remain "machines" or if they will be able to become companions. Will people begin to say, as they do, about people who have "met their dog" that someone has "met her robot"? Would such a person still feel shame in front of the robot if they had that kind of relationship with it? Is there still a need to discuss the robot's "moral standing" at that point of personal engagement? Isn't moral quality implicit in the very relationship that has emerged here? For example, suppose an older person is already very attached to her Paro robot and treats it as a pet or baby. In that case, that relationship must be discussed rather than the robot's "moral standing."

The personal encounter with the Other, *i.e.,* the robot, is central to this relational and phenomenological approach. Personhood as a relational concept can be fleshed out in the following ways:

A social model of autonomy in which autonomy is defined in the context of social relations rather than individually.

- Personhood is absolute and inherent in every entity as a social being; it is not gradable.

- A non-cognitivist integrationist model of personhood in which personhood is relational by nature (but not necessarily reciprocal) and defined in non-cognitivist terms.

The preceding claims are not intended to be steps in a conclusive argument; rather, they depict the general line of reasoning regarding the moral significance of social relations. The relational approach does not necessitate that the robot is rational, intelligent, or autonomous as an individual entity; rather, the social encounter with the robot is morally decisive. The robot's moral standing is founded on this social encounter.

The problem with the relational approach is that robots' moral status is thus entirely dependent on human willingness to engage in social relations with a robot. In other words, if humans do not want to enter such relationships for whatever reason, they may deny robots the moral status to which they may be entitled, based on more objective criteria such as rationality and sentience. Consequently, the relational approach does not offer a solid basis for robot rights; rather, it promotes a pragmatic perspective that makes it easier to accept robots (who already have moral standing) into the moral community (Gordon 2020c).

iv. The Upshot

The most important observation is that robots, once they have met the relevant criteria, are entitled to moral status and rights regardless of our opinion. It remains to be seen whether humans will recognise their status and rights.

Value Alignment and the Singularity

Some of the theories discussed about the potential moral status of artificial intelligent agents have struck some authors as science fiction. The same can be said about the next topic under discussion: singularity. I. J. Good, a statistician, introduced the underlying argument for technological singularity in 'Speculations Concerning the First Ultra intelligent Machine' (1965):

Let us define an ultra-intelligent machine as one that can outperform all the intellectual activities of any man, no matter how clever. Because machine design is one of these intellectual activities, an ultra-intelligent machine could design even better machines; there would undoubtedly be an "intelligence explosion," and human intelligence would be far behind. As a result, the first ultra-intelligent machine is the last invention that man will ever need to make.

Many people find the notion of a self-replicating, super-intelligent AI machine causing an intelligence explosion incomprehensible, and other pundits reject such assertions as a fiction regarding AI's future growth (for example, Floridi 2016). However, prominent voices both within and outside academia are taking this concept seriously—to the point of becoming worried about the possible consequences of so-called "existential risks," such as the danger of human extinction. Philosophers like Nick Bostrom and Toby Ord and public figures like Elon Musk and the late Stephen Hawking have expressed similar concerns.

The authors who have written about the concept of technological singularity have different ideas about what might lead to it. Ray Kurzweil is well-known for advocating the idea of singularity with exponentially increasing computing power, which is associated with 'Moore's law,' which states that, at the time of writing, the computing power of transistors had been doubling every two years since the 1970s and could reasonably be expected to continue to do so in the future (Kurzweil 2005). According to this viewpoint, the path to superintelligence will most likely be paved with continuous hardware improvement. Another viewpoint on what might lead to superintelligence, advocated by well-known AI researcher Stuart Russell, focuses on algorithms. According to Russell (2019), conceptual breakthroughs in areas such as language and common-sense processing and learning processes are required for singularity to occur.

Singularity researchers approach the question of what to do to protect humanity from such existential risks in various ways, depending on what they believe these existential risks are based on. For example, Bostrom defines superintelligence as a maximally powerful capacity to achieve whatever goals are associated with artificial intelligent systems. In his well-known example (Bostrom 2014), a super-intelligent machine threatens the future of human life by becoming optimally efficient at maximising the number of paper clips in the world, a goal that could be aided by removing humans to make more space for paper clips. From this perspective, it is critical to provide super-intelligent AI machines with the right goals, so that when they pursue these goals in the most efficient ways possible, they do not extinguish the human race along the way.

This is one way to consider how to create a useful super-intelligence.

Russell (2019) takes an alternative approach, proposing three AI design principles that may be seen as an updated version of or replacement for Asimov's fictional robotics laws:

- The machine's sole goal is to maximise the realisation of human preferences
- The machine is initially unsure of what those preferences are
- Human behaviour is the ultimate source of information about human preferences

The theories discussed in this section represent various perspectives on what is sometimes referred to as 'value alignment,' or the idea that the goals and operations of AI systems, particularly super-intelligent future AI systems, should be properly aligned with human values. According to the ideal of value alignment, AI should track human interests and values, and its operation should benefit us rather than pose any existential risks. As stated at the outset of this section, some commentators believe that the idea of AI becoming super-intelligent and posing existential threats is simply a myth that needs to be debunked. Others, such as Toby Ord, believe that AI is one of the primary reasons why humanity is in a critical period in which its very survival is at stake. According to such assessments, AI should be treated on par with nuclear weapons and other potentially highly destructive technologies that, unless properly valued, put us all at risk.

A key issue with value alignment, especially when viewed through the lens of Russell's three principles, is determining whose values or preferences AI should be aligned with. As Iason Gabriel (2020) points out, reasonable people may disagree on which values and interests to align AI's operation with (whether super-intelligent or not). Gabriel's solution to this problem is based on John Rawls' (1999, 2001) work on 'reasonable pluralism.' Rawls proposes that society seeks to identify "fair principles" that can generate overlapping consensus or widespread agreement despite the existence of more specific, reasonable disagreements about values among society members. But how likely is it that such convergence in general principles will be widely supported?

OTHER DISCUSSIONS ABOUT THE ETHICS OF ARTIFICIAL INTELLIGENCE

In addition to the topics mentioned above, other issues that have received less attention are beginning to be discussed within the context of AI ethics. Five of these issues are briefly discussed below.

i. Artificial intelligence as a form of moral enhancement or a moral advisor

AI systems are commonly used as 'recommender systems' in online shopping, online entertainment (such as music and movie streaming), and other areas. Some ethicists have debated the benefits and drawbacks of AI systems whose recommendations could assist us in making better decisions that are more consistent with our core values. Perhaps, in the future, AI systems will be able to assist us in improving our values. Borenstein and Arkin (2016), Giubilini *et al.* (2015, 2018), Klincewicz (2016), and O'Neill *et al.* (2017) have all published papers on these and related topics (2021).

ii. Artificial Intelligence and the Future of Work

Much debate about AI and the future of work revolves around the critical question of whether AI and other forms of automation will result in widespread "technological unemployment" by eliminating large numbers of human jobs that would be replaced by automated machines (Danaher 2019a).

This is frequently presented as a negative prospect, with the question of how and whether a world without work would provide people with any opportunities for fulfilling and meaningful activities because certain goods obtained through work (other than income) are difficult to obtain in other contexts. Some authors, however, have argued that work in the modern world exposes many people to various types of harm (Anderson 2017).

Danaher (2019a) investigates the critical question of whether a world with less work is preferable. Some argue that if humans can no longer find a meaningful purpose in their work (or even in their lives) because machines have replaced them, existential boredom will spread (Bloch 1954). On the other hand, Bloch is criticised by Jonas (1984), who claims that boredom will not be a significant issue. Another related issue, which may be more pressing in the short and medium term, is how we can ensure that increasingly technologised work remains meaningful.

iii. Artificial Intelligence and the Future of Personal Relationships

Various AI-driven technologies influence the nature of friendships, romances, and other interpersonal relationships, and they may have a greater impact in the future. Online 'friendships' arranged through social media have been studied by philosophers who disagree on whether relationships curated in part by AI algorithms can be considered true friendships. Some philosophers have harshly criticised AI-powered dating apps, fearing that they will reinforce negative stereotypes and gender expectations. In more science-fiction-like philosophising, which may yet become more prevalent in real life, there has also been debate about whether humans could have true friendships or romantic relationships with robots and other artificial agents equipped with advanced AI.

iv. AI and the Concern About Human 'Enfeeblement.'

Suppose AI recommendations drive more and more aspects of our lives (because we don't understand how it works and may question its propriety). In that case, the results could include a "crisis in moral agency" (Danaher 2019d), human "enfeeblement" (Russell 2019), or "de-skilling" in various areas of human life (Vallor 2015, 2016). This scenario becomes even more likely if technological singularity is attained because, at that point, intelligent machines could do all work, including research and engineering. After a few generations, humans may be completely reliant on machines in all aspects of life, unable to turn back the clock. This is a very dangerous situation, so it is critical that humans maintain their skills and knowledge while developing AI capabilities.

v. Anthropomorphism

According to some, the very concept of artificial intelligent machines that mimic human thinking and behaviour may involve a form of anthropomorphism that should be avoided. In other words, a problem may arise if we attribute humanlike characteristics to machines that are not human. Many people are concerned that many types of AI technologies (or how they are presented to the general public) are deceptive. Many people have complained that companies exaggerate the extent to which their products rely on AI technology. For example, several prominent AI researchers and ethicists have chastised the creators of Sophia the robot for portraying her as far more humanlike than she is and designing her to elicit anthropomorphising responses in humans that are problematic or inappropriate. The related question of whether anthropomorphising responses to AI technologies are always problematic requires more thought.

49

This list of emerging AI ethics topics is not exhaustive, as the field is very fertile, with new issues arising regularly. This is possibly the most rapidly growing area of study in the field of ethics and moral philosophy.

CHAPTER FIVE
ETHICAL CHALLENGES OF ARTIFICIAL INTELLIGENCE

Artificial intelligence is now used in various industries, including healthcare, retail, manufacturing, and even government. However, there are ethical issues with AI, and we must remain vigilant about these issues to ensure that artificial intelligence does not cause more harm than good.

Here are some of the most serious ethical issues confronting artificial intelligence.

Biases

We need data to train our AI algorithms, and we must do everything possible to eliminate bias in that data.

The ImageNet database, for example, has significantly more white faces than non-white faces. When we train our AI algorithms to identify facial characteristics using a database that isn't balanced enough, the system will perform badly on non-white faces, resulting in a built-in bias that may have a major effect. To counter this argument, the majority of the population in the USA is however white (58%). In other countries, surveillance databases are trained specifically on the minority groups to get greater accuracy differentiating those in such minority groups, so even the reporting can be biased!

Rather than shrugging our shoulders and if we're training AI to properly represent our culture, I think it's essential that we remove as much prejudice as possible when training AI. This work starts with being aware of the possibility of bias in our AI solutions.

Control and the Morality of Artificial Intelligence

We are expecting machines to make more critical choices as

we utilise artificial intelligence more and more. For example, there is currently an international convention governing the use of self-driving drones. If you have a drone that can launch a rocket and kill someone, a human must be involved in the decision-making process before the missile is launched. So far, a patchwork of rules and regulations like this has circumvented some of AI's critical control problems.

The problem is that AIs are being asked to make split-second decisions more often. In high-frequency trading, for example, over 90% of all financial trades are now controlled by algorithms, thus putting a person in charge of the decisions is impossible. They can only set guiding parameters.

The same is true for self-driving cars. If a child runs out on the road, they must act quickly, so the AI must be in command of the situation. This raises interesting ethical questions about AI and control as detailed in chapter four above.

Privacy

Privacy (and consent) for data use has long been an ethical quandary in AI. To train AIs, we need data, but where do we obtain it, and how do we utilise it? We often presume that all data is collected from individuals with full mental capabilities who can make their own choices about how to use it, but this is not always the case.

Barbie, for example, now has an AI-enabled doll that children can converse with. In terms of ethics, what does this imply? An algorithm is collecting data from your child's interactions with this toy. What happens to this data, and how is it used?

There are many companies that collect data and sell it to other companies, as we have seen in the news recently. What are the rules governing this type of data collection, and what legislation may be required to protect users' private information?

Power Balance

Amazon, Facebook, Microsoft and Google are using artificial intelligence to crush their competitors and become virtually unstoppable in the market. Countries such as China have ambitious AI strategies that the government backs - funding at a rate which almost matches the rest of the world combined. *"Whoever wins the AI race will very certainly become the world's ruler,"* once stated Russian President Vladimir Putin.

How can we ensure that the monopolies we create distribute wealth fairly and that we don't have a few countries that race ahead of the rest of the world? In the world of artificial intelligence, balancing that power is a significant challenge.

Ownership

Who is to blame for some of the things that AIs create? Artificial intelligence may now be used to generate misleading text, bots, and even deepfake videos. Who owns that content, and what do we do if it spreads across the internet?

We also have AIs capable of producing art and music. Who owns a new piece of music composed by an AI? Who owns the intellectual property rights to it, and who should be compensated for it?

Environmental Impact

We don't always consider the environmental impact of AI. We assume that we are training an algorithm on a cloud computer and then using that data to run recommendation engines on our website. However, the computer centres that power our cloud infrastructure consume a lot of power.

AI training, for example, can produce 17 times the carbon

emissions that the average American does in a year. How can we harness this energy for the greater good and use AI to solve some of the world's most pressing issues? If we are only using artificial intelligence for its sake, we may need to reconsider our options.

Humanity

"How does AI make us feel as humans?" is my final challenge. Artificial intelligence has advanced to the point where it is so fast, powerful, and efficient that it can make humans feel inferior. This issue continues to accelerate exponentially and so may force us to reconsider what it means to be human.

In the future, AI will continue to automate more of our occupations. What will be our human contribution? Artificial intelligence, in my opinion, will never be able to replace all our jobs, but it will be able to supplement them. We must improve our ability to collaborate with intelligent machines to manage the transition with dignity and respect for both people and technology.

These are some of the major ethical issues that we must all consider carefully when it comes to AI.

CHAPTER SIX
BIO-INSPIRED COMPUTING

Bio-inspired computing is a research method that solves problems by using computer models based on biological and natural world principles. Bio-inspired computing, which is commonly regarded as a philosophical approach, is used in several related fields of study within computing rather than as a field of study in and of itself. Bio-inspired computing is a subset of the closely related field of biomimicry.

Bio-inspired computing prioritizes tractability and dependability over-optimised, high-speed algorithms. In general, the approach is built from the ground up, rather than building on a large foundation of knowledge. Bio-inspired computing frequently starts with a small set of rules and builds on them with unsupervised deep learning in training.

When there is no clear solution to a problem, a useful change of perspective can provide a new opportunity for solutions. A good question to ask is, "Does this problem have any natural parallels?" If the answer is "yes," that parallel can be studied to find similar parallels in solutions. This philosophy has proven to be useful in resolving a wide range of issues.

Examples of bio-inspired computing applications

Examples of bio-inspired computing can be found frequently in AI, particularly in machine learning, where biological organisms' learning processes can be emulated. Among the applications of bio-inspired computing are:

- Robot design
- Learning classifier systems
- Sensory networks
- Excitable media
- Membrane computers

- Network communications and protocols
- Linden Mayer systems
- Graphics rendering
- Artificial immune systems
- Artificial life
- Emergent systems
- Cellular automata
- Biodegradability prediction
- Neural networks
- Genetic algorithms

AIMS OF BIO-INSPIRED COMPUTING

- Gives biologists an IT-oriented paradigm for studying how cells 'compute' or process information.
- Assists computer scientists and engineers in the development of natural-systems-based algorithms such as evolutionary and genetic algorithms.

EXAMPLES OF BIO-INSPIRED COMPUTING

- Swarm intelligence (for example, DECENTRALISED ROBOTS)
- Neural networks
- Evolutionary Computation (*e.g.,* GENETIC ALGORITHM)
- Ant Colony Management
- Immune-inspired computer/network security
- Molecular terms (DNA COMPUTATION)

CURRENT ISSUES IN BIO-INSPIRED COMPUTING

Despite the popularity and success of Swarm intelligence (SI) and bio-inspired computing, many difficult issues remain. We focus on five issues here: gaps between theory and practice, classifications, parameter tuning, a lack of truly large-scale real-world applications, and algorithm selection.

Discrepancies between Theory and Practice

In bio-inspired computing, there is a significant gap between theory and practice. Nature-inspired metaheuristic algorithms appear to work almost magically in practice, but it is unclear why. For example, except for a few genetic algorithms, simulated annealing, and particle swarm optimisation, there aren't many good results in metaheuristic algorithm convergence analysis and stability. A lack of theoretical understanding may hinder progress or even create resistance to wider applications of meta-heuristics.

Theoretical analysis of algorithms can be divided into three categories: complexity theory, dynamical systems, and Markov chains. On the one hand, metaheuristic algorithms have low algorithm complexity, but can solve extremely complex problems. Complexity analysis is an active research area that necessitates more in-depth examination.

Conversely, convergence analysis typically employs dynamic systems and statistical methods based on Markov chains. For example, Clerc and Kennedy (2002) investigated particle swarm optimisation using simple dynamic systems, whereas genetic algorithms were extensively investigated in a few theoretical studies. For example, the number of iterations in genetic algorithms can be estimated for a given mutation rate (p), string-length (L), and population size (n) by

$$t \leq \left\lceil \frac{\ln(1-p)}{\ln\{1 - \min[(1-\mu)^{L_n}, \mu^{L_n}]\}} \right\rceil$$

Where denotes the largest integer value of u, and p is a function of L and n. Theoretical understanding lags, and thus there is a strong need for additional research in this area.

There is no doubt that any new understanding will better understand how metaheuristic algorithms work.

Terminology and classifications

There are several methods for categorising optimisation algorithms; one of the most common is based on the number of agents, while another is based on the iteration procedure. The former will result in two types of agents: single agents and multiple agents. Simulated annealing is a single-agent algorithm that follows a zigzag piecewise trajectory, whereas genetic algorithms, particle swarm optimisation, and the firefly algorithm are population-based algorithms. These algorithms frequently have multiple agents interacting in a nonlinear fashion, and a subset of these is known as a SI-based algorithm. Particle swarm optimisation and the firefly algorithm, for example, are swarm-based algorithms inspired by the swarming behavior of birds, fish, and fireflies or by SI in general.

Another method of classifying algorithms is based on the algorithm's core procedure. If the procedure is fixed and without any randomness, an algorithm that starts from a given initial value will always reach the same final value, regardless of when it is run. This is referred to as deterministic. The classic Newton–Raphson method, for example, is a deterministic algorithm, as is the hill-climbing method, *i.e.* it works its way iteratively to the optimal result. On the other hand, an algorithm contains some randomness in its procedure; it is referred to as stochastic, evolutionary, heuristic, or even metaheuristic. Genetic algorithms with mutation and crossover components, for example, can be referred to as evolutionary algorithms, stochastic algorithms, or metaheuristic algorithms.

These various names for algorithms with stochastic components reflect a problem that still exists in the terminologies and terms used in the current literature. Before the 1980s, algorithms such as genetic algorithms were referred to as evolutionary algorithms; now, they can be referred to as both evolutionary-based and metaheuristic. There are bio-inspired algorithms, nature-inspired algorithms, and metaheuristics in general, depending on the source of inspiration. Recent trends, however, refer to such algorithms as "metaheuristic."

In a nutshell, heuristic means "by trial and error," and metaheuristic is a higher-level method that employs specific selection mechanisms and information sharing. Glover is credited with coining the term "metaheuristic" (1986). Multiple names and inconsistencies in terminologies in the literature necessitate efforts from research communities to agree on some common terminologies and systematically classify and analyze algorithms. The current dramatic growth in the literature makes it an even more difficult task.

We attempted to use metaheuristic, SI, and bio-inspired computation in the appropriate contexts in this chapter, focusing on metaheuristics. It is worth noting that algorithms can be classified as either local or global in terms of mobility. Local search algorithms typically converge toward a local optimum rather than the global optimum, and such algorithms are frequently deterministic, with no ability to escape local optima, as with the simple hill-climbing algorithm. On the other hand, we always try to find the global optimum for a given problem, and if this global optimality is robust, it is often the best, though this global optimality is not always possible to find. Local search algorithms are unsuitable for global optimisation. We must employ a global search algorithm. Modern metaheuristic algorithms are designed for global optimisation in most cases, though they are not always successful or efficient.

Algorithm-Dependent Parameter Tuning

All metaheuristic algorithms have algorithm-dependent parameters, and the appropriate setting of these parameter values significantly impacts an algorithm's performance. Choosing which parameter values to use in an algorithm is one of the most difficult issues. How can these parameters be optimised to improve the performance of the algorithm of interest?

Parameter tuning is a difficult optimisation problem in and of itself. There are two main approaches in the literature. One method is to run an algorithm with some trial values of key parameters to obtain a good set of these parameters. These parameters are then set for more extensive test runs with the same or larger problems. The other approach is to use one algorithm (which may be well tested and established) to tune the parameters of a newer algorithm. Then a critical issue arises. What tool or algorithm should we use to tune algorithm A if we use algorithm A (or tool A) to tune algorithm B? What tool should we use to tune algorithm C if we use, say, algorithm C to tune algorithm A? In fact, these critical issues are still being researched.

The requirement for large-scale and real-world applications

SI and bio-inspired computation are extremely effective at solving a wide range of practical problems. However, in terms of the number of design variables, the size of these problems is small to moderate. Studies have focused on design problems with a dozen or fewer variables in the current literature, with a maximum of a hundred. It is unusual to come across studies with hundreds of variables. On the other hand, Linear programming routinely solves design problems with half a million to several million design variables. As a result, applying Si-based algorithms to real-world, large-scale problems remains a huge challenge.

A methodology issue accompanies this challenge. Nobody knows whether we can directly apply methods that work well for small-scale problems to large-scale problems. Aside from size differences, there may be other issues such as memory capacity, computational efficiency, and computing resources that require special attention. What are our options if we cannot effectively extend existing methods to deal with large-scale problems, which is often the case? After all, real-world problems are frequently nonlinear and on a large scale. Such techniques can be used to tune home automation or machine tool settings, because these problem spaces are already constrained. More in-depth research is desperately needed in this area.

Choice of Algorithms

Even with all the knowledge and books on optimisation and algorithms, most readers are unsure which algorithms to use. It's like going to a shopping mall to select a product. There are frequently numerous options, and making the best choice is yet another optimization problem. There is no agreed-upon guideline for selecting algorithms in the literature, though there are specific instructions on using a specific algorithm and what types of problems it can solve. As a result, the issue of choice remains partly based on experience, partly on trial and error.

Even with the best of intentions, the availability of an algorithm and the expertise of the decision-makers are sometimes the deciding factors when selecting an algorithm. Even if some algorithms are superior to others for the given problem, we may not have that algorithm implemented in our system or have access to it, limiting our options. Many software packages implement Newton's method, hill-climbing, Nelder–Mead downhill simplex, trust-region methods, and interior-point methods, which may increase their popularity in applications. In practice, even with the best algorithms and well-crafted implementations, we may not achieve the desired results.

This is the nature of nonlinear global optimisation, as many of such problems are NP-hard, and no efficient algorithm (in the polynomial-time sense) exists for any given problem. Thus, the challenges of research in computational optimisation and applications are finding the best algorithms for a given problem to obtain good solutions, hopefully also the best solutions in the world, in a reasonable timescale with limited resources.

AI AND BIO-INSPIRED COMPUTING

Bio-inspired computing differs from traditional artificial intelligence (AI) in that it uses a more evolutionary approach to learning rather than what could be described as 'creationist' methods used in traditional AI. In traditional AI, intelligence is frequently programmed from on high: the programmer creates something and imbues it with intelligence. Bio-inspired computing, on the other hand, takes a more bottom-up, decentralised approach; bio-inspired techniques frequently involve the method of specifying a set of simple rules, a set of simple organisms that adhere to those rules, and a method of applying those rules iteratively.

It is common for some forms of complex behaviour to emerge after several generations of rule application. Complexity builds on complexity until the result is something noticeably complex and quite often completely counterintuitive to what the original rules would have produced. As a result, it is necessary for neural network models to accurately model an *in vivo* network by collecting "noise" coefficients in real-time that can be used to refine statistical inference and extrapolation as system complexity increases.

Natural evolution is a good analogy for this method–the rules of evolution (selection, recombination/reproduction, mutation, and, more recently, transposition) are, in theory, simple rules, but they have produced remarkably complex organisms over thousands of years. In genetic algorithms, a similar technique is used.

CHAPTER SEVEN
AUGMENTED INTELLIGENCE

Artificial Intelligence (AI) clearly has a bright future in the world of technology, with the potential to disrupt virtually every industry. Tech companies are beginning to view AI in a new light, realising that combining human and AI capabilities can result in greater business value. So, what is Augmented Intelligence? Augmented intelligence (AI), also known as intelligence augmentation (IA), cognitive augmentation, decision support, machine augmented intelligence and enhanced intelligence. While Artificial Intelligence is the creation of machines that operate and respond like people, Augmented Intelligence is the use of the same machines to help human workers. Indeed, Augmented Intelligence entails humans and machines collaborating to maximise business value by playing to their respective strengths. In other words, the primary goal of IA is to enable humans to work more efficiently and effectively.

WHY SHOULD YOU BE INFORMED ABOUT ENHANCED INTELLIGENCE?

"Augmented Intelligence is the key to driving rapid business value with AI," says Kjell Carlsson, Ph.D., Senior Analyst at Forrester. According to Kjell, *"companies that are making headway with Artificial Intelligence, that are quickly driving new business value and have results to show for it, are usually using AI technologies to make an employee's life better…Augmented Intelligence is usually a better approach than using AI to replace human intelligence,"* he concludes.

In recent years, Augmented Intelligence has been ranked second in AI technology rankings regarding the value it creates for businesses, just below virtual agents. According to Gartner, *"decision support and AI augmentation will exceed all other kinds of AI efforts"* this year, then explode by 2025, becoming nearly twice as valuable as virtual agents.

WHAT IS AUGMENTED INTELLIGENCE, AND HOW DOES IT WORK?

Augmented Intelligence platforms can collect all types of data (structured and unstructured) from various sources across disparate and siloed systems and present that data in a way that provides human workers with a complete 360-degree view of each customer. The insight derived from that data and presented to the user is more profound and comprehensive than ever before. As a result, workers are better informed about what is going on in their industry, how it may affect their customers, and what opportunities or threats may arise. The combination of this wealth of data with the human touch is what makes this technology so effective.

USE CASES OF AUGMENTED INTELLIGENCE

Although it is still in its early stages, IA has already had a positive impact on a variety of industries, and the nature of this technology, which learns faster, adapts faster, and improves over time, means that early adopters gain an advantage.

Augmented Intelligence systems can transform how all businesses interact with their customers throughout the customer life cycle, including onboarding, advisory services, and customer support. Let's look at some potential applications in various industries:

Financial services:

Assisting financial planners in providing customized services based on the customer's goals, capacity, and risk tolerance.

Healthcare:

Improving patient care and lowering the likelihood of

medical errors while speeding up time-consuming procedures such as billing and claims.

Retail:

Increasing shopper engagement and conversion by allowing online shoppers to shop the way they think by leveraging machine cognition of their declared, observed, and inferred behaviours.

Travel:

During travel, improve customer complaint response, interaction, and feedback analysis.

Manufacturing:

Assisting and accelerating the generative design process, in which a human worker enters parameters, and the machine generates a plethora of designs for the object. The machine investigates a plethora of options in record time, and the human applies their expertise to choose the best option, delivering value to customers and increasing efficiency.

Oil and gas:

Precision drilling in the oil and gas industry. The human worker can better understand the environment in which they work, resulting in faster results and less wear, tear, and damage to machinery. The possibilities are endless, but the unifying thread is obviously improving worker knowledge to improve efficiency. *"To minimize the dangers of decision automation, the aim is to be more efficient with automation while supplementing it with a human touch and common sense,"* says Ms. Sicular, research vice president at Gartner.

The aim of Augmented Intelligence systems is to enhance any user's work, knowledge, and experience, from a consumer to a field worker to a CEO, by arming them with machines that continuously access, interpret, apply, and learn from the meaning buried within all types of data.

WORKING WITH MACHINES FOR ABSTRACT TASKS AND ROBOTICS

As we enter the Second Machine Age, where AI, Machine Learning, and Robotics technologies are increasingly influencing this revolution, significant automation changes occur in many industries, including warehousing and distribution centers. Many jobs in these industries are not only being transformed but are also being partially or fully automated, frequently replacing the lowest skilled workers.

EXAMPLES OF ARTIFICIAL INTELLIGENCE IN EVERYDAY LIFE

In pop culture, examples of artificial intelligence (AI) usually involve a horde of intelligent robots bent on eradicating humanity, or at the very least a fancy theme park. Sentient machines with general artificial intelligence do not yet exist and are unlikely to exist shortly, so we're safe... for the time being.

That is not to dismiss AI's potential impact on our future. According to a recent poll, more than 72% of Americans are concerned about a future in which machines perform many human tasks. Furthermore, tech billionaire Elon Musk, a long-time supporter of AI regulation, recently declared AI to be more dangerous than nuclear weapons. Despite these valid concerns, we are still a long way from living in Westworld.

Artificial intelligence is all around us, whether we know it or not, and it is very much a part of our everyday life. Every time we check our Facebook newsfeed, browse the web, receive an Amazon product recommendation, or book a vacation online, AI is working in the background. Leaders in the robotics industry are still unable to agree on what the term "robot" entails. Roboticists define robots as programmable machines that perform tasks, but no one knows where that definition ends.

Today's AI-powered robots, or at least those deemed to be such, still lack natural general intelligence, but they can solve problems and "think" in a limited capacity. Examples of artificial intelligence in robotics range from working on assembly lines at Tesla to teaching Japanese students English.

Companies that use robotics as part of their AI strategy include:

iRobot

iRobot, the makers of the popular Roomba, is back with a new, much smarter robotic vacuum. The Roomba 980 model employs artificial intelligence to scan a room, identify obstacles, and remember the most efficient cleaning routes. The self-deploying Roomba can also determine how much vacuuming is required based on the size of the room, and it does not require human assistance to clean floors.

In 2017, the company completed its first year as a purely consumer-focused business, earning $883.9 million in revenue, and has shipped over 10 million Roombas since 2002.

Hanson Robotics

Hanson Robotics designs and manufactures humanoid robots with artificial intelligence for both the commercial and consumer markets. Sophia – referred to above, created by Hanson, is an extremely advanced social-learning robot. Sophia can communicate effectively with natural language and use facial expressions to convey human-like emotions thanks to AI.

Sophia became something of a media celebrity in recent

years, appearing on a variety of talk shows, including a memorable appearance on The Tonight Show with a clearly weirded-out Jimmy Fallon. Saudi Arabian citizenship has even been granted to the robot.

Hanson plans to produce a complete line of Sophia-like robots, thinking that they would *"have immediate uses as media personalities in films and television programs, entertainment animatronics in museums and theme parks, and for university research and medical training applications."*

Emotech

Emotech created Olly, a voice-controlled AI assistant like Amazon Alexa or Google Home, but with one major difference: Olly has a changing personality. Olly's personality is derived from a combination of machine learning algorithms that teach the robot to become more like its owner over time.

Emotech's AI-powered technology can recognise a user's facial expressions, voice inflections, and verbal patterns to initiate conversations and make relevant suggestions. The small, robotic table-top assistant can also move and will orient itself toward the user when deciding what to do next.

Olly's abilities far exceed what current voice assistants are capable of. If Olly notices you resting your head, it may enquire if you've had a long day and then recommend some of your favorite music to help you unwind.

Healthcare

Artificial intelligence is proving to be a game-changer in healthcare, improving nearly every aspect of the industry, from robot-assisted surgeries to protecting private records from cybercriminals.

Spiraling medical costs and inefficient processes have long

plagued healthcare. The maligned industry is getting a much-needed makeover thanks to artificial intelligence.

Here are a few examples of how artificial intelligence streamlines processes and creates innovative new opportunities in the healthcare industry.

Covera Health

Covera Health is reducing the number of misdiagnosed patients worldwide by leveraging collaborative data sharing and applied clinical analysis. The company's proprietary technology uses a framework that combines advanced data science and artificial intelligence to sort through existing diagnostics and provide practitioners with more accurate symptom data when making a decision that has a significant impact on a patient's life, reducing the cascading effects of misguided care and potentially saving the healthcare industry hundreds of billions of dollars.

Well

Well enables people to live better lives and receive medical advice more quickly, allowing them to make more informed decisions about their care. Well helps individuals choose the appropriate health path for them based on their pre-existing conditions, current health concerns, and knowledge gaps in general health. It is powered by a proprietary AI-driven "health engine" that helps personalize health guidance to each user. The health engine combines personal and external health data to provide informed advice based on other users' experiences, as well as points that can be redeemed at stores for completing challenges and supporting communities, assisting users with everything from screenings and questionnaires to prescription support, vaccination advice, recommended doctor's visits, and specific condition guidance.

PathAI

PathAI develops artificial intelligence-powered technology for pathologists. Pathologists can use the company's machine learning algorithms to analyse tissue samples and make more accurate diagnoses. The goal is to improve not only diagnostic accuracy but also treatment. PathAI's technology can also select the best clinical trial participants.

PathAI collaborated with the Bill & Melinda Gates Foundation and Philips to create high-volume prognostic test support tools and plans for long-term access to their advanced diagnostic services.

Pager

Pager employs artificial intelligence to assist patients suffering from minor aches, pains, and illnesses. Machine learning is used by the company to analyse clinical and claims data to identify gaps in a patient's healthcare treatment. In addition to making healthcare recommendations, this concierge-style service assists patients in scheduling appointments and making payments. The Pager app allows users to text a nurse 24/7, video chat with a doctor, and have prescriptions filled as needed.

Atomwise

Atomwise uses AI and deep learning to help in drug development. *"Extract insights from millions of experimental affinity measurements and thousands of protein structures to forecast the binding of tiny compounds to proteins,"* according to Atomwise's algorithms, which are based on convolutional neural networks.

The company's AI has increased hit rates by 10,000 times and screens 10 to 20 million compounds per day, while identifying patient characteristics for clinical trials. The ability to analyze billions of compounds and identify areas for drug discovery is rapidly speeding up chemists' work.

Atomwise is being used to combat some of today's most pressing medical issues, such as Ebola and multiple sclerosis.

Massachusetts General Hospital (MGH)

One of the world's oldest institutions, Massachusetts General Hospital, has teamed up with computing giant NVIDIA to deploy AI-powered machines for disease detection, diagnosis, treatment, and management. To enable quicker testing and diagnostic skills, the programs are presently training with more than 10 billion medical images in radiology and pathology.

The hospital recently completed a pilot system that used artificial intelligence to quickly prescreen patients for pneumothorax, also known as a collapsed lung. The results were promising enough that plans are in the works to implement the technology in the emergency room.

Self-Driving Cars

Self-driving cars are the ultimate indicator that the future has arrived. Self-driving technology, which was once considered science fiction, is gradually making its way towards a driverless reality. In fact, by 2040, it is expected that more than 33 million autonomous vehicles will be on the road. We can thank artificial intelligence for the advancements we see in this truly futuristic technology package.

The future of self-driving cars is literally being driven by artificial intelligence. These cars are equipped with sensors that continuously monitor what is going on in their environment and utilize artificial intelligence to make the required changes. Thousands of data points (such as vehicle speed, road conditions, pedestrian location, other traffic, and so on) are captured every millisecond by these sensors, which are then interpreted and acted upon by AI in the blink of an eye. Before

72

we can completely autonomously drive, we may still have a long way to go.

Motional

Motional is leveraging advanced AI and machine learning technology to make driverless vehicles safer, more reliable, and more accessible. The company was formed through a collaboration between Apertiv, an automotive technology company, and the Hyundai Motor Group, who combined their expertise in functional and forward-thinking technology to create better driverless technology that is adaptable in the present rather than the future.

Since 2016, Motional has supplied more than 100,000 self-driven rides, while maintaining a record of zero at-fault incidents by combining short-range and long-range LiDAR sensors, radar, strategic camera placement, and proprietary tech in development. The company has begun collaborating with major rideshare companies such as Lyft, Via, and Cox Automotive to bring its technology to a larger scale, with rollouts beginning as early as 2021.

Cruise

Cruise is at the forefront of self-driving technology. The company's self-driving vehicles are among the world's first to hit the road, with AI guiding the way. Every day, self-driving cars collect a petabyte's worth of data. This massive data set is used by AI to constantly learn about the best safety measures, driving techniques, most efficient routes, and so on to provide the rider with the ultimate assurance that they are safe.

Cruise is currently using artificial intelligence to power their self-driving cars and their "Cruise Origin"- a self-driving electric shared vehicle. The futuristic-looking vehicle has traveled over a million miles in San Francisco alone without involving a single 'fender bender'.

Waymo

Google's self-driving car project is known as Waymo. The company makes a variety of AVS to suit the requirements of people, rideshare drivers, and big freight companies throughout the nation.

Waymo's cars have already logged millions of kilometers across ten states, gathering and analyzing data using AI. Thanks to a sophisticated array of sensors, each Waymo car gathers data and utilises artificial intelligence to anticipate what will happen next. Thanks to artificial intelligence (AI), Waymo cars can evaluate circumstances and make safe predictions for optimum future actions without ever needing a person to engage with the steering wheel.

The company's ride-hailing service, Waymo One, is now being utilized in the Phoenix area to pick up riders and carry them autonomously to their destinations. Waymo Via, on the other hand, focuses on autonomous vehicles for long-distance logistics and last-mile delivery.

Luminar Technologies

Luminar Technologies manufactures one of the world's most advanced LIDAR-based vehicle vision products. The company's sensors use fiber lasers to provide an in-depth view of the world around a self-driving car's AI system. The technology enables artificial intelligence-based software systems to see people, objects, events, road conditions, and so on from more than 250 meters away, allowing an autonomous vehicle to analyze and react to any given situation. The innovative technology can measure the speeds of various objects, allowing an AV to easily determine its most optimal move in a safe amount of time.

Finance

AI and the finance industry are a perfect match. To make decisions, the financial sector relies on accuracy, real-time reporting, and the processing of large amounts of quantitative data, all of which intelligent machines excel at.

Automation, chatbots, adaptive intelligence, algorithmic trading, and machine learning are all being quickly integrated into financial operations as the industry realizes AI's efficiency and accuracy.

The robo-advisor, or automated portfolio manager, is one of the most significant financial trends of 2018. These automated advisors use artificial intelligence and algorithms to scan market data and predict the best stock or portfolio based on preferences. Wealth management firms are turning to robo-advisors to save time and money for both the company and the client and produce some extraordinary returns.

Betterment

Betterment is a digital financial investing platform and a pioneer of robo-advisor technology, which uses artificial intelligence to learn about an investor and create a personalized profile based on his or her financial goals.

Betterment's robo-advisors use algorithms to automate tax-loss harvesting, trading, transactions, and portfolio management, all of which used to take a lot of human effort and knowledge. Betterment has $10 billion in assets under management and 250,000 customers as of last year.

AlphaSense

AlphaSense developed an AI-powered financial search engine to assist investment firms in gaining a competitive information advantage. The program can analyze key data points from 35,000 financial institutions using a combination of linguistic search and natural language processing. The ability of the system to scan millions of data points and generate actionable reports based on relevant financial data saves analysts countless hours of work.

Numerai

Numerai is an AI-powered hedge fund that uses crowdsourced machine learning from thousands of data scientists worldwide. The company makes abstracted financial data available to its community of data scientists, who use various machine learning models to forecast the stock market.

The models compete in a weekly tournament for Numeraire (NMR), the company's cryptocurrency, in which creators compete for Numeraire (NMR). The most accurate predictions reach the top of the leaderboard and are rewarded with more tokens.

However, Numerai isn't about rewarding winners and losers. The competition is simply a means of amassing more models. The real breakthrough for the company is how it combines all the different approaches into a "Meta Model."

The diversity of the models within the "Meta Model" generates diversity in the portfolio, lowering risk and increasing returns. Simply put, the more algorithms that are in play, the better.

Transportation and Travel

Artificial intelligence is becoming a major trend in the travel and transportation sectors. From arranging travel reservations to suggesting the most efficient way home after work, AI is making it easier to move about.

Travel companies are benefiting from the widespread use of smartphones. More than 70% of users say they use their phones to book trips, read travel tips, and look up local landmarks and restaurants. One in every three people has used a virtual travel assistant to plan a future trip.

AI-powered chatbots are transforming the travel business by allowing customers to interact with them in a human-like manner, resulting in quicker response times, lower booking costs, and even travel recommendations.

For instance, telling a travel chatbot you want to go to Paris may result in a natural language response recommending flights, hotels, and things to do in the City of Light based on the user's preferences gleaned from the conversation.

Here are some examples of artificial intelligence in the travel and transportation industries.

Google

Google uses AI in various applications, but its specific application in Google Maps makes our commutes a little easier. The search giant's AI-enabled mapping technology scans road information and uses algorithms to determine the best route to take, whether on foot, in a car, bike, bus, or train.

Google intends to advance artificial intelligence in the Maps app soon by incorporating its voice assistant and creating real-time augmented reality maps. In addition to assisting millions of users every day, the popular ridesharing service Lyft built its navigation features for drivers using Google Maps.

Hopper

Hopper uses artificial intelligence to predict when you

should be able to book the best deals on flights, hotels, car rentals, and vacation home rentals. Hundreds of bookings are scanned by the company's AI, which then shows the most current pricing. But there's a lot more to this artificial intelligence than meets the eye.

Hopper will also offer suggestions to the user based on a previous flight and hotel data, such as whether the booking has hit its lowest price point or whether the customer should wait for the price to decrease a bit longer. Hopper's AI-based system has already saved customers over $2.2 billion in in-flight expenses.

Hipmunk

Concur's Hipmunk offers booking prices for flights, hotels, excursions, and even vacation rentals through Airbnb. "Hello Hipmunk," which debuted in 2015, is an AI-powered travel assistant.

Users can book flights and vacation ideas based on themes and interests by chatting with the bot on Facebook or Slack. Travelers can also include "Hello Hipmunk" in an email discussing potential travel plans, and the bot will provide travel recommendations. Furthermore, the virtual assistant will your calendar for upcoming events and start planning a future trip.

"Hello Hipmunk" was one of the first travel chatbots, and it remains popular more than two years later. Overall, the virtual assistant industry is rapidly expanding, with total revenue expected to reach $15.8 billion by 2021.

Social Media

With over 2.77 billion active profiles across platforms such as Twitter, Facebook, and Snapchat, social media is constantly fighting to personalize and cultivate meaningful experiences for users. Artificial intelligence has the potential to make or break the industry's future. Because of its capacity to organise huge quantities of data, recognise images, create chatbots, and anticipate cultural changes, AI is very useful to an industry with billions of users and $45 billion in annual revenue.

Furthermore, in an industry under pressure to regulate false news, hate speech, and other bad actors in real-time, advanced machine learning will almost likely be essential.

Here are a few instances of how artificial intelligence is being used by some of the game's biggest names.

Facebook (Meta)

AI is deeply embedded in Facebook's platform, whether it's Messenger chatbots, algorithmic newsfeeds, photo tagging suggestions, or ad targeting. The company's artificial intelligence team has trained an image recognition model to 85 percent accuracy using billions of public Instagram pictures labeled with hashtags. The method represents a significant advancement in computer vision modeling.

Facebook is already combating spam and abuse with a combination of artificial intelligence and human moderation. With improvements in image recognition and a doubling-down on AI research, Facebook is relying on artificial intelligence to help it regulate the world's biggest media platform.

Twitter

You can thank artificial intelligence for the tweets you see on Twitter. The social media behemoth's algorithms suggest that users follow tweets and news based on their own interests. Furthermore, Twitter employs artificial intelligence to monitor and categorise video feeds based on topic. AI is also used in the company's image cropping tool to determine how to crop images to focus on the most interesting part.

Twitter's artificial intelligence was recently put to work identifying hate speech and terroristic language in tweets. The company identified and banned 300,000 terrorist-linked accounts in the first half of 2017, with non-human, artificially intelligent computers identifying 95 % of them.

Slack

Slack's AI gathers information on how each company and its employees use the tool and interact with one another using a data structure known as the "work graph."

Data from the "work graph" can then be used to train artificial intelligence models that improve the usability of Slack. For example, the company estimates that the average user receives more than 70 messages per day. Slack's "Highlights" feature employs machine learning and natural language processing to push more relevant messages to the top.

In addition to "Highlights," Slack's search feature uses artificial intelligence to help users find knowledge specialists and the channels where they can be contacted based on a study of who is talking about what and where.

E-Commerce

Have you ever been scrolling through a website only to see an image of the same shirt you were looking at on another site pop up again? That can be attributed to artificial intelligence.

Companies can build personal relationships with their customers by incorporating machine learning into their e-commerce processes. AI-powered algorithms personalize the user experience, increase sales, and foster long-term relationships.

Artificial intelligence is used by businesses to deploy chatbots, predict purchases, and collect data to create a more customer-centric e-commerce experience. Here's how some of the world's largest e-commerce companies use AI to increase sales and loyalty.

Amazon

Amazon is the undisputed king of e-commerce AI. Amazon uses artificial intelligence in almost every step of its process, whether it's product recommendations, warehouse robots that grab, sort, and ship products, or web services that power the website itself.

Alexa, the company's AI-powered voice assistant, was introduced in 2014. Alexa, inspired by the computers on Star Trek, ushered in a new era of powerful, conversational virtual assistants.

With a slew of AI projects, Amazon has practically rebuilt its business on artificial intelligence. Simply put, if you've purchased anything from Amazon in the last five years, an algorithm has assisted you.

Twiggle

Twiggle, an advanced e-commerce search engine, uses natural language processing to improve businesses' search relevance and product awareness.

The combination of human-like deep learning and a retail industry understanding helps customers find exactly what they need.

According to Twiggle, a site with two million visitors per month could lose up to 266,600 customers due to poor search results. Customers who use its search benefit from a 9% increase in "add to cart" and a 12% increase in click-through rate.

Marketing

Marketers are assigning an increasing portion of their budgets to artificial intelligence implementation because machine learning has many applications for successfully managing marketing campaigns.

Another justification for the budget increase? AI-enabled tools are now widely available to small and medium-sized businesses.

Artificial intelligence is assisting marketers in creating in-depth customer insight reports, powering relevant content creation, and booking more impactful business meetings — all without relying heavily on humans.

Here are a few examples of how artificial intelligence is being used in marketing.

Grammarly

Grammarly works in the same way that an editor would if they were reviewing your writing in real-time. Okay, Grammarly can't replace an editor, but it can help clearer and more correct everyone's writing.

Amplero

Amplero creates artificial intelligence-powered marketing tools for various consumer-facing industries, including finance, retail, telecommunications, and gaming. The algorithms used by Amplero detect patterns in data to create dynamic audience profiles. Marketers can then run thousands of experiments at scale using the company's software and machine learning capabilities.

In one case study, a company that used Amplero to boost upsell, reduced its acquisition cost from $40 to $1 and saw an 88 percent increase in average revenue per postpaid customer.

The company's AI tools are used by major brands such as Sprint, Microsoft, and TaxAct.

Drift

Drift helps companies schedule more meetings, answer customer questions about products, and shorten the sales cycle by using chatbots, machine learning, and natural language processing.

The technology excels at automating previously time-consuming marketing tasks. For example, if a customer visits a Drift-powered website, a chatbot will appear, ask questions, and automatically enroll them in a campaign if they are a lead. Furthermore, the company's "Drift Assistant" automates email responses, lead routing, and contact information updates.

Drift is being used by companies such as Toast and Zenefits to fulfill quality sales leads in minutes rather than days. Over 100,000 businesses now use drift.

CHAPTER EIGHT
ROBOTIC PROCESS AUTOMATION (RPA): THE FUTURE DIGITAL WORKFORCE

Robotic Process Automation (RPA) represents a new wave of future technologies. Robotic Process Automation is cutting-edge technology in the fields of computer science, electronics and communications, mechanical engineering, and information technology. It is a combination of hardware and software, networking, and automation for performing simple tasks.

J. Presper Eckert and John Mauchly invented the ENIAC computing machine at the University of Pennsylvania in 1943, but it was not completed until 1946. According to some, the abacus was the first computing machine, however **Colossus** was a set of computers developed and used by British codebreakers in the years 1943–1945 in secret, to help in the cryptanalysis of the Lorenz cypher.

This is how the computing era began decades ago. Computing technology, like a chameleon, is changing colours in terms of hardware such as desktops, servers, laptops, mobiles, and now "rolltops." Furthermore, there has been a lot of software development at the networking edge level with high bandwidth in terms of operating systems, programs, utilities, and computational capabilities. Furthermore, organisational applications, such as punch cards, spreadsheets, office applications, management information systems, and enterprise resource planning have stepped into various folds to help in business applications. Nowadays, business operations are advancing into a new technological realm known as "Robotic Process Automation."

As a result, the year "2018" is known as the "Robotic Process Automation" year. Industry entering the new world of technology "Robotic Process Automation." known as "RPA."

The timely implementation of RPA has become a requirement in day-to-day business operations. Companies that do not incorporate this technology into their operations risk failing to compete soon. Robotic process automation (RPA) is a new type of business process automation technology that is based on software robots or artificial intelligence (AI) workers. RPA has emerged as the new business language. This cutting-edge technology is more powerful than other twenty-first-century technologies.

New hardware, software, and smart devices will significantly aid the way businesses do business. Human lifestyles are changing worldwide because of global collaborations, multinational businesses, and new IT/ITes advancements with RPA technology. Along with the existing new technologies that are functional in human life, such as Viz.

On the Internet of Things, Big Data Analytics, Deep Learning, Artificial Intelligence, Machine Learning, and other related technologies, RPA is becoming a significant disruptive technology. According to the literature, Human-Robot Interaction (HRI) and robot companionship positively affect the human psychological state when used to address a lack of human resources. Fortune 500 companies, as well as new start-ups, are therefore conducting extensive research on Robotic Process Automation. The following section defines Robots, Automation, and RPA specifics.

"Robotics" is an interdisciplinary area of engineering and science that includes electrical engineering, computer science, mechanical engineering, and other fields. Robots are electromechanically constructed machines that may be programmed by a computer and execute complicated tasks autonomously. A robot moves about in the actual world to perform tasks. The perception-to-action linkages in these robots are 'intelligent'. Artificial Intelligence must play a key role if the link is to be intelligent (Brady, 1985).

Sophia, referred to above, is a social humanoid robot developed by Hanson Robotics in Hong Kong. Sophia was activated on April 19, 2015 (Harriet Taylor, 2016) and made her first public appearance in mid-March 2016 at the Southwest Festival (SXSW) in Austin, Texas. According to Jump up (2018), Sophia can display more than 50 different facial expressions. According to Gershgorn (2017), experts who have reviewed the robot's open-source code believe Sophia is best classified as a Chabot with a face.

In recent years, the robotics industry has been booming. By 2020, 10% of major businesses in supply-chain-dependent sectors hired a chief robotics officer to oversee their operations. Robotics are artificial intelligence devices that are frequently used in manufacturing units. Robots use shared resources such as wireless networking, big data, cloud computing, statistical machine learning, open-source, and other shared resources to improve performance in a variety of applications such as assembly, inspection, driving, warehouse logistics, caregiving, package delivery, housekeeping, and surgery. Swarm robotics is a novel approach to coordinating large groups of relatively simple robots that social insects inspire.

Evolutionary robotics, according to Palgrave et al. (2000), is a novel method for the automated development of autonomous robots. This technique, which is based on the Darwinian principle of selective reproduction of the fittest, considers robots to be autonomous artificial organisms that develop their skills through close interaction with the environment without human intervention. Ambient robotics focuses on the physical and informational co-adaptation and compatibility of assistive environments and service robot systems. A 3D graphics assist facility planners in visualising the system before construction, make alternative designs, program robot paths, obtain system layouts, obtain data for the discrete event simulation, and develop the cell control program. In the not-too-distant future, robots will be a part of human society.

Process

The term "process" is well-known to everyone and is even associated with people's daily lives and is spread across all sectors. It is a necessary component of any system or firm and is the activity used to complete a task. People, things, or a combination of both can complete the process. Regardless of whether the system is closed or open, the process accepts input from various devices or people and executes the predefined rules to produce the desired output.

The process is simply the conversion of input to output. However, the time required, the cost incurred, the workforce required, and other quality parameters differ from process to process and system to system. People are familiar with various process systems, including biological, manufacturing, chemical, admission, and many others. Consider a computer processor system as an example. It accepts keyboard, joystick, mouse, and even voice recognition input. It performs tasks using the central processing unit (CPU) or graphics processing unit (GPU) as directed and displays the results on the screen, printer, or invoice format.

The processing is carried out with the assistance of single/multiple core processors to carry out single/multiple tasks simultaneously. Companies in today's advanced computing environment have cutting-edge technologies to perform concurrent processes quickly and accurately within the specified constraints. All smart devices have the most recent hardware, software, personal digital assistants, and advanced processors such as Intel Core I3 - I7 8th Gen (Coffee Lake) and AMD Ryzen 3 and 5 with RX Vega 11 Graphics. That is why, even in the exceptional technology "Robotic Process Automation," process/processors are critical tasks.

Automation

The technique of making an apparatus, a process, or a system operate automatically is known as "automation." However, society is already reaping the benefits of automation applications in daily life. Any system's processing capability is included in automation. It is not easy to integrate people and systems to achieve automation. Human factors, particularly cognitive aspects, are frequently misunderstood and overlooked in system design.

A system for creating, editing, running, monitoring, and debugging an application program for controlling an industrial automation mechanism includes logic, motion, and process control components. Curb energy is a home energy management system. Some of the most recent home automated smart devices include Ecobee3 Smart Wi-Fi Thermostats, Sonos Wireless Speaker systems, Philips Hue Smart Light Bulbs, BelkinWeMo Switch, and Motion Sensor Amazon Echo device Alexa, and Lutron Dimmer Light Switches. These smart devices complete tasks on their using embedded software and hardware. The best part about these smart devices is that they improve people's quality of life, increase operational efficiency, and handle situations where human intervention is impossible.

The automation process makes daily life easier, faster, and better, and it even frees humans from the labour and monotony of repetitive tasks. Some of the most advanced automation technologies used in the automotive industry are machine vision and artificial intelligence for driverless/autonomous vehicles. Cognitive Computing in Internet of Things Connected Cars and Collaborative Robots Automation is already in use in the manufacturing sector, most notably in the form of "Industry 4.0" technology. Assembly lines with robots doing most of the work are becoming a reality.

Robotic Process Automation

The term "Robotic Process Automation" conjures up images of physical robots roaming around offices performing human tasks; however, the term refers to the automation of service tasks that humans previously performed.

Robotic automation is the use of specific technology and methodologies to operate a computer or robot. Instead of a person, a virtualised FTE or robot will manipulate existing application software Enterprise Resource Planning, claims applications, databases, and learning management systems in the same way that a person currently processes a transaction or completes a process.

In 2016, there was a significant increase in the use of robotic process automation in back offices and shared service operations and among BPO service providers themselves. Robotic Process Automation (RPA) is progressing from pilot projects to widespread adoption. The Pronexus Interactive Voice Response (IVR) development toolkit provides basic information to customers while connecting them to the appropriate call center executive. The term was coined by David Moss and Alastair Bathgate of M/s Blue Prism in the United Kingdom "Automation of Robotic Processes."

With new v6 features and integrations, Blue Prism provides an intelligent, connected, and simple-to-use digital workforce. RPA is the use of software to perform tasks that humans previously performed. Because it replaces human resources, software is viewed as a robot. RPA, when combined with artificial intelligence, can be used to aid in the handling of unstructured data in support of fraud / anti-money laundering (AML).

Blue Prisms' digital labor allows Shop Direct, Co-operative Banking Group, Fidelity Investments, RWE Npower, the

NHS, and O2 to react quickly to business change via flexible back-office operations and is fueling the outsourcing industry's next big revolution. RPA is an emerging technology that is being used by more CIOs to streamline enterprise operations and reduce costs. According to experts, RPA can help businesses automate mundane rules-based business processes, allowing business users to devote more time to serving customers or other higher-value work. Companies are increasing productivity by deploying software robots to carry out routine, rules-based service processes. If done correctly, such automation can lead to high-performing human-robot teams in which software robots and human employees complement one another.

Simply stated, Robotic Process Automation (RPA) is the automation of repetitive and rule-based activities using non-invasive software called BOT that can imitate human behaviours on computers to accomplish different business processes (K.V.N. Rajesh *et al.,* 2018). Regardless, *"Despite the fact that the name 'Robotic Process Automation' conjures up visions of actual robots wandering about workplaces doing human jobs, RPA is a software-based solution... A One software license is equivalent to "robot" in RPA lingo."*

RPA tools, according to Gartner, are at the "peak of inflated expectations" in the so-called Hype Cycle (Kerremans, 2018). For the past 10-15 years, software tools for automated regression testing and automated performance monitoring using virtual users from various locations have been available. These tools could simulate human workers and perform repeatable tasks such as regression testing and monitoring of various front-end desktop and online applications. RPA is a logical progression of these functions.

RPA products are available from Automation Edge, Automation Anywhere, Blue Prism, Cognizant, Conduent, Kofax, Kryon Systems, Pegasystems, Soft motive, and UiPath, to name a few. Software robots will replace a significant proportion of white-collar employment, just as physical robots have quickly replaced industrial, blue-collar professions. As a result, the Robotic Process Automation specialist must be aware of the RPA software orientation in terms of installation, structure (Flowchart *vs.* Sequence), control flow (Decisions, Loops, Switches), error handling with Try/Catch, automating excel, word, and Portable Document File interactions, automating email and attachments, decomposing a process into reusable sub-components, and debugging skills, among other things.

Outside of routine processes, robotics can generate high-quality responses to more complex questions. AI techniques enable software to digest massive amounts of research on a wide range of topics — far more research than any human could.

When asked about the outlook for the Chinese stock market by a client, a "The "chatbot" could have compiled all the pertinent data and responded that there was a consensus that the Chinese stock market would rise. In fact, digital competitors are increasingly putting pressure on financial advisors "Robo-Advisers." According to Brandon Buccowich (2016) of M/s. Laserfiche, the Robotic Process Automation technology, has many benefits such as improving employee morale, increasing productivity, ensuring low technical barriers, compliance, consistency leading to reliability, and being non-invasive. This expert discussed the benefits of RPA in detail in a seminal, as shown in the diagram below.

Even non-technical workers can design their software robots to tackle automation problems, which is the beauty of robot process automation technology. Payroll, employee status changes, new hire recruiting and onboarding, accounts receivable and payable, invoice processing, inventory management, report generation, software installs, data transfer, and vendor onboarding, to name a few, may all benefit from RPA.

CHAPTER NINE
ARTIFICIAL INTELLIGENCE AND
MACHINE LEARNING

We can now compute the immensity of space and the minute intricacies of subatomic particles thanks to computers. Computers surpass humans when it comes to counting and calculating, as well as following logical yes/no algorithms, thanks to electrons flowing at the speed of light via its circuitry. However, we do not generally regard them as "intelligent" because, historically, computers have not been able to do anything without being taught (programmed) by us first.

Even if a computer had access to all the world's knowledge, it could not do anything "clever" with it thus far. If we tell it that images included cats, it could locate one for us. In other words, if you ask it to find a picture of a cat, it will return a picture of a cat that it has been told is a picture of a cat.

This has several implications that limit its usefulness, not the least of which is that a significant amount of human time must be spent telling it what each picture contains. The data (pictures) must pass through a human bottleneck, where they are labeled before the computer can identify it as a cat picture and show it to us when we ask for it.

While this works well enough for searching for cat pictures on Google to pass the time, it falls short when we want to do something more advanced, such as to monitor a live video feed and alert us when a cat walks in front of the camera.

This is the type of problem that machine learning is attempting to solve. At its most basic, machine learning (ML) is the process of teaching computers to learn in the same way that humans do, by interpreting data from their surroundings, classifying it, and learning from their successes and failures. In fact, machine learning is a subset of artificial intelligence, or, to put it another way, the cutting edge of artificial intelligence.

How did machine learning emerge?

Building algorithms capable of doing so, using computers' binary "yes" and "no" logic, is the foundation of machine learning – a phrase probably coined by Arthur Samuel at IBM during serious research in the 1950s. Samuel's first experiments entailed teaching machines to play checkers.

Because knowledge is so fundamental to learning and a foundation for making decisions, knowledge is something to draw insight from, a lack of data severely hampered these early computers. Without all the digital technology we have today to collect and store information from the analog world, machines could only learn from data slowly entered via punch cards and, subsequently, magnetic tapes and storage.

Today, we have more data than we know what to do with due to the growth of the internet, the proliferation of mobile, data-gathering phones and other gadgets, and the adoption of online, linked technologies in business.

No human brain can hope to process even a small portion of the digital information available to it. Could a computer, with its lightning-fast speed and infallible binary logic, do it?

Deep learning and neural networks

The notion that it can is one-half of what is driving today's game-changing breakthroughs. The other half is machine learning's "brain." Because, to learn, a machine must process data in addition to ingesting it.

Several frameworks have been tested over the years when developing algorithms to allow machines to deal with data in the same way humans do. These frequently drew on statistics, employing linear regression and sampling methods to assign probabilities to various outcomes, making predictions. However, the artificial neural network framework has surpassed all others in popularity in recent years by consistently demonstrating its usefulness and adaptability.

By incorporating neuroscience into the equation, researchers discovered that computer models that appear to function more like a human brain than anything previously developed was possible. Artificial neural networks, like real brains, are made up of interconnected "neurons" that are all capable of performing a data-related task – such as recognising something, failing to recognise it, matching a piece of information to another piece of information, and answering a question about their relationship.

Each neuron can send the results of its work to a neighboring neuron, which can then process it further. Because the network can change and adapt based on the data that passes through it to deal with the next bit of data more efficiently, it can be thought of as "learning" in the same way that our brains do.

Another popular buzzword is "deep learning," which is simply machine learning derived from "deep" neural nets. To allow a more sophisticated simulation of human learning, these are built by stacking several networks on top of one another and routing input via a tangled web of algorithms. Because of the growing power and decreasing price of computer processors, machines with the grunt to operate these networks are becoming more affordable.

What can machine learning be used for?

Machine learning's use in society and industry leads to advancements in a broad variety of human activities. In medicine, for example, machine learning is being applied to genomic data to help doctors understand and predict how cancer spreads, allowing for the development of more effective treatments.

Data from deep space is being collected here on Earth via massive radio telescopes – and after being analysed with machine learning, it is assisting us in unraveling the mysteries of black holes.

Machine learning in retail matches shoppers with products they want to buy online, and it allows shop assistants to personalise the service they provide to their customers in the brick-and-mortar world. Machine learning is used in the war on terror and extremism to predict the behaviour of those who wish to harm the innocent.

Now machine learning powers Google's search and image algorithms in our daily lives, allowing us to be more accurately matched with the information we need when we need it. Natural language processing (NLP) allows computers to understand and communicate with us in human language through machine learning. It has resulted in breakthroughs in translation technology and the voice-controlled devices we increasingly use every day, such as Amazon's Echo.

Without a doubt, machine learning is demonstrating that it is a transformative technology. In many areas, robots capable of working alongside humans and complementing our creativity and imagination with their perfect logic and superhuman speed are no longer a science fantasy dream. The key that has unlocked it is machine learning, and the potential for future applications are almost endless.

WHAT IS THE DIFFERENCE BETWEEN ARTIFICIAL INTELLIGENCE AND MACHINE LEARNING?

Artificial Intelligence (AI) and Machine Learning (ML) are both very popular expressions, and they frequently appear to be used interchangeably. They aren't the same thing, but the perception that they are can cause some confusion. So, I thought it would be worthwhile to write a piece to explain the distinction.

Both terms frequently appear when discussing Big Data, analytics, and the broader waves of technological change that are sweeping our world.

In a nutshell, artificial intelligence is the broader concept of machines being able to perform tasks in a way that we would consider "smart." And Machine Learning is a current AI application based on the idea that we should be able to simply give machines access to data and let them learn for themselves. Different machine learning techniques abound, including 'Deep Learning' using neural networks.

Early Days

Artificial intelligence has been around for a long time – Greek myths tell of mechanical men who mimic our behaviour. Early European computers were conceived of as "logical machines," and engineers saw their job as attempting to create mechanical brains by reproducing capabilities such as basic arithmetic and memory.

As technology and, more importantly, our understanding of how our minds work has advanced, so has our understanding of what constitutes AI. Rather than increasingly complex calculations, AI research has focused on mimicking human decision-making processes and carrying out tasks in increasingly human-like ways.

Artificial Intelligence – devices designed to act intelligently – are frequently divided into two broad categories: applied and general. Applied AI is far more common; for example, 'narrow AI systems' described previously, designed to intelligently trade stocks and shares, or maneuver an autonomous vehicle fall into this category.

Generalized AIs – systems or devices that can theoretically handle any task – are less common, but they are where some of the most exciting developments are taking place today. It is also the field that has given rise to Machine Learning. It's more accurate to think of it as the current state-of-the-art rather than a subset of AI.

The rise of Machine Learning

Two significant breakthroughs resulted in the emergence of Machine Learning as the vehicle that is propelling AI development at the current rate. One of these was Arthur Samuel's 1959 realisation that, rather than teaching computers everything they need to know about the world and how to perform tasks, it might be possible to teach them to learn for themselves.

The second, more recent, was the advent of the internet, which resulted in a massive increase in the amount of digital information generated, stored, and made available for analysis. Engineers realised that instead of teaching computers and robots how to do everything, it would be much more efficient to program them to think like humans and then link them to the internet so they could access all the world's information.

Neural Networks

The development of neural networks has been critical in teaching computers to think and understand the world in the same way we do while retaining the inherent advantages that computers have over us, such as speed, accuracy, and lack of bias.

A Neural Network is a computer system that is designed to classify information in the same way that the human brain does. It can be taught to recognise and classify images, for example, based on the elements they contain.

It essentially operates on a probability system – based on data fed to it, it can make statements, decisions, or predictions with a high degree of certainty. The addition of a feedback loop allows for "learning" – by sensing or being told whether its decisions are correct or incorrect, it modifies its approach in the future.

Machine Learning applications can read text and determine whether the author is complaining or congratulating themselves. They can also listen to music and determine whether it is likely to make someone happy or sad, and then find other music to match the mood. In some cases, they can even compose their music that expresses the same themes as the original piece or that they know will be appreciated by fans of the original piece.

All of these are possibilities provided by systems based on machine learning and neural networks. The idea that we should be able to communicate and interact with electronic devices and digital information as naturally as possible with another human being has also emerged, thanks in no small part to science fiction. To that end, another branch of AI, Natural Language Processing (NLP), has emerged as a source of tremendously exciting innovation in recent years, and it is heavily reliant on ML.

NLP applications attempt to understand natural human communication, whether written or spoken, and then communicate with us in a similar, natural language. ML is used here to assist machines in understanding the vast nuances of human language and learning to respond in a way that a specific audience is likely to understand.

A case of branding?

Artificial intelligence – and specifically, machine learning (ML) – has a lot to offer. With its promise of automating mundane tasks while also providing creative insight, industries ranging from banking to healthcare and manufacturing benefit. So, keep in mind that AI and ML are something else... they are products that are being sold – consistently and profitably.

Marketers have undoubtedly recognised Machine Learning as an opportunity. After AI has been around for so long, it's possible that it's become an "old hat" even before its full potential has been realised. There have been a few false starts on the road to the "AI revolution," and the term Machine Learning certainly offers marketers something new, shiny, and, most importantly, firmly grounded in the here-and-now.

Technologists have frequently regarded the eventual development of human-like AI as a foregone conclusion. Certainly, we are closer than ever before, and we are accelerating our progress toward that goal. Much of the exciting progress in recent years has been attributed to fundamental changes in how we envision AI working, which have been brought about by ML.

CHAPTER TEN
USING AI TO IMPROVE HUMAN INTERACTION

People interact with one another in a variety of ways. In fact, few people realise how many ways communication takes place. Many people associate communication with either writing or speaking. On the other hand, interaction can take many different forms, including eye contact, tonal quality, and even scent. The electronic nose, which relies on a combination of electronics, biochemistry, and artificial intelligence to perform its task and has been applied to a wide range of industrial applications and research, is an example of a computerised version of enhanced human interaction. This chapter, on the other hand, focuses on standard communication, including body language.

Understanding how artificial intelligence can improve human communication in less expensive ways than building an electronic nose may help. AI can also improve the way people exchange ideas. In some cases, AI provides entirely new modes of communication, but in many cases, AI provides a subtle (or not-so-subtle) method of enhancing existing modes of communication. Humans rely on exchanging ideas to create new technologies, improve existing technologies, or learn about technologies required to increase an individual's knowledge. Because ideas are abstract, exchanging them can be difficult at times, so AI can provide a much-needed bridge between people.

Previously, if someone wanted to save their knowledge to share with others, they would generally rely on writing. In some cases, they could also supplement their communication with various types of graphics. However, only some people can use these two types of media to learn new things; many people need more, which is why online sources like YouTube have grown in popularity. Surprisingly, you can use AI to augment the already significant power of multimedia, and this chapter explains how.

The final section of this chapter explains how an AI can provide you with near-superhuman sensory perception. Perhaps you need that electronic nose after all. It provides significant advantages in detecting scents that are significantly less aromatic than humans can detect. Consider being able to smell at the same level as a dog (which uses 100 million aroma receptors versus the 1 million aroma receptors that humans possess). It turns out that there are two ways to accomplish this goal: using monitors that a human can access indirectly and direct stimulation of human sensory perception.

DEVELOPING NEW WAYS TO COMMUNICATE

Communication involving a developed language initially took place between humans via the spoken versus written word. The only issue with spoken communication is that the two parties must be close enough to each other to talk. As a result, written communication is superior in many ways because it allows for time-delayed communications that do not necessitate the two parties ever seeing each other. Human nonverbal communication is based on three main methods:

- **Alphabets:** The abstraction of human word or symbol components.

- **Language:** The combination of words or symbols to form sentences or convey ideas in written form.

- **Body language:** The addition of context to language.

The first two methods are straightforward abstractions of spoken words. They are not always simple to put into practice, but people have been doing so for thousands of years. Because you're attempting to create an abstraction of a physical process, the body-language component is the most difficult to implement. Using specific terminology, writing aids in the communication of body language. However, the written word falls short, so people supplement it with symbols such as *emoticons* and *emojis*.

Making up new alphabets

This section's introduction discusses these new alphabets popular in the computer age: emoticons. There are hundreds of websites where you can find these two graphic alphabets. Humans can generally interpret these iconic alphabets because they resemble facial expressions, but because an application lacks the human sense of art, computers frequently require AI just to figure out what emotion a human is attempting to convey with the little pictures. Fortunately, standardised lists are available, such as the Unicode emoji chart, which can be found at https://unicode.org/emoji/charts/full-emoji-list.html. Of course, a standardised list does not aid in translation.

If you don't want to sift through the 2,666 official emoji supported by Unicode, you can use Dango (a mobile app) to suggest an appropriate emoji for you.

Since the beginning of the written word, humans have created new alphabets to meet specific needs. Emoticons and emojis are just two of the many alphabets that humans will create due to the Internet and the use of AI. In fact, keeping up with them all may necessitate the use of artificial intelligence.

AUTOMATING LANGUAGE TRANSLATION

The lack of a common language has always been a problem for the world. Yes, English has become universal — to a point — but it is still far from universal. Having someone translate between languages can be costly, time-consuming, and error-prone, so translators aren't always the best solution, when necessary, in many situations. Dealing with other languages can be difficult for those who do not have the assistance of a translator, which is where applications like *Google Translate* come in.

One thing to keep in mind is that Google Translate can automatically detect the language for you. What's intriguing about this feature is that it works extremely well in most cases. The Google Neural Machine Translation (GNMT) system is responsible for this feature. It can analyse entire sentences to make sense of them and provide better translations than applications that rely on phrases or words as the basis for translation.

What's more, GNMT can use an artificial language, an interlingua, to translate between languages even when it doesn't have a specific translator. However, it's important to understand that an interlingua isn't a universal translator; rather, it's a universal bridge. Assume the GNMT is unable to translate between Chinese and Spanish. It can, however, translate between Chinese and English as well as English and Spanish. GNMT can create its translation between Chinese and Spanish by creating a 3-D network representing these three languages (the interlingua). Unfortunately, this system will not work for translating between Chinese and Martian because no method for understanding and translating Martian in any other human language is currently available. Humans must still create a base translation for GNMT to function.

Incorporating body language

Body language plays an important role in human communication, so emoticons and emojis are so popular. On the other hand, people are becoming more accustomed to working directly with cameras to create videos and other forms of communication that do not require writing. In this case, a computer could listen to human input, parse it into tokens representing human speech, and then process those tokens to fulfill a request, like how Alexa, Google Home, and other similar devices work. Unfortunately, simply translating spoken words into tokens will not suffice because the issue of nonverbal communication remains. In this case, the AI must be able to directly read body language. Body language reading entails interpreting the following human characteristics:

- Posture
- Head movement
- Facial expression
- Eye contact
- Gestures

Of course, there are other factors to consider, but if an AI can master these five areas, it will be well on its way to providing accurate body-language interpretation. In addition to body language, current AI implementations consider tonal quality, resulting in an extremely complex AI that still doesn't come close to doing what the human brain does seemingly effortlessly.

When an AI can read body language, it must also be able to output it when interacting with humans. Because reading is still in its infancy, robotic or graphic representations of body language are even less developed. Because robots are currently incapable of producing natural-looking facial expressions, the best-case scenario is to substitute posture, head motion, and gestures for body language. The result isn't particularly impressive.

EXCHANGE OF IDEAS

An AI lacks ideas because it lacks both intrapersonal intelligence and understanding. On the other hand, an AI can enable humans to exchange ideas in ways that result in a whole that is greater than the sum of its parts. In many cases, the AI isn't engaging in any sort of transaction. The exchange is carried out by the humans involved in the process, who rely on AI to augment the communication process. The sections that follow go into greater detail about how this process works.

Establishing connections

A human can exchange ideas with another human, but only if the two humans are aware of each other. The issue is that many experts in one field don't know each other — at least not well enough to communicate. An AI can conduct research based on the flow of ideas provided by a human and then connect with other humans who have the same (or similar) flow of ideas.

One way in which this communication is created is through social media sites such as LinkedIn, where the goal is to connect people based on a variety of criteria. A person's network serves as a conduit for the AI deep within LinkedIn to suggest other potential connections.

Augmenting Communication

Two humans must be able to communicate effectively to successfully exchange ideas. The only problem is that humans don't always communicate well, and they don't always communicate at all. The problem isn't just one of translating words; it's also one of translating ideas. Individuals' societal and personal biases can obstruct communication because an idea for one group may not translate at all for another. For example, laws in one country may cause someone to think one way, but laws in another country may cause the same person to think in an entirely different way.

In theory, an AI could aid communication between disparate groups in a variety of ways. Language translation is, of course, one of these methods (assuming the translation is accurate). However, by prescreening materials, an AI could provide cues as to what is and isn't culturally acceptable. An AI could use categorization to suggest aids such as alternative graphics and so on to help communication take place in a way that benefits both parties.

Identifying trends

Humans frequently base their ideas on trends. However, to visualise how the idea works, other participants in the exchange must also see those trends and communicating with this information is notoriously difficult. AI can perform various levels of data analysis and graphically present the results. The AI can analyse data in more ways and faster than a human, ensuring that the story the data tells is the one you want it to tell. The data is the same; the presentation and interpretation of the data are different.

According to studies, humans relate better to graphical output than to tabular output, and graphical output will undoubtedly make trends more visible. Tabular data is typically used to present only specific information; graphics are always best for displaying trends. Using AI-powered applications can also make it easier to create the right type of graphic output for a specific requirement. Because not all humans perceive graphics in the same way, matching a graphic type to your audience is critical.

Making Use of Multimedia

Most people learn by employing a variety of senses and approaches. A learning pathway that works for one person may be completely perplexing to another.

As a result, the more ways a person can communicate concepts and ideas, the more likely other people will understand what the person is attempting to communicate. Multimedia typically consists of sound, graphics, text, and animation, but some multimedia performs additional functions.

AI can assist with multimedia in a variety of ways. One of the most important is in multimedia creation or authoring. AI can be found in applications ranging from media development to media presentation. For example, when translating the colors in an image, an AI may be able to help you visualize the effects of those changes faster than if you tried one colour combination at a time (the brute-force approach).

Following the use of multimedia to present ideas in multiple forms, those receiving the ideas must process the information. A secondary application of AI is the use of neural networks to process data in various ways. Today, categorising multimedia is an essential use of technology. However, in the future, AI will be used to assist in the 3-D reconstruction of scenes based on 2-D images. Consider the possibility of police officers being able to walk through a virtual crime scene, with every detail faithfully captured.

People used to speculate that different types of multimedia would emerge in new forms. Consider a newspaper that features dynamic displays reminiscent of Harry Potter. Most of the technology is already available, but the issue is one of market availability. To be successful, technology must have a market —a way to pay for itself.

EMBELLISHING HUMAN SENSORY PERCEPTION

One way AI truly excels at improving human interaction is by augmenting humans in one of two ways: using their natural senses to work with augmented data or augmenting the native senses to do more. The sections that follow go over both approaches to improving human sensing and, as a result, communication.

Shifting data spectrum

When gathering various types of information, humans frequently use technologies that filter or shift the data spectrum in terms of color, sound, or smell. The human continues to use native capabilities, but some technology modifies the input so that it works with that native capability.

One of the most common applications of spectrum shifting is in astronomy, where shifting and filtering light allows people to see astronomical elements, such as nebulae, in ways that the naked eye cannot, thereby improving our understanding of the universe.

However, manually shifting and filtering colors, sounds, and smells can take a long time, and the results can be disappointing even when done expertly, which is where AI comes in. Because an AI performs the task in a consistent manner, it can try various combinations far faster than a human and locate potentially useful combinations with greater ease.

Augmenting human senses

You can augment human senses as an alternative to using an external application to shift data spectrum and somehow make that shifted data available for use by humans. A device, either external or implanted, enables a human to directly process sensory input in a new way in augmentation. Many people believe that these new abilities will lead to the creation of cyborgs.

The concept is not new: use tools to make humans more effective at a variety of tasks. Humans are augmented in two ways in this scenario: physically and intellectually.

Physical augmentation of human senses already occurs in various ways and is only going to become more prevalent as humans become more receptive to various types of implants. Night vision glasses, for example, currently allow humans to see at night, with high-end models offering color vision controlled by a specially designed processor. In the future, eye augmentation/replacement may allow people to see any part of the spectrum as controlled by thought, allowing them to see only the part of the spectrum required to perform a specific task. Intelligence Augmentation necessitates more intrusive measures, but it also promises to provide humans with far greater capabilities. In contrast to AI, Intelligence Augmentation (IA) places a human actor at the centre of the processing. Humans provide the creativity and intent that AI presently lacks.

CHAPTER ELEVEN
USING ARTIFICIAL INTELLIGENCE (AI)
IN YOUR BUSINESS

Most businesses are swimming in data right now, but less than 1% of that data is being used at all, let alone analysed for meaningful decision-making.

There is no doubt that your organisation will need to become more intelligent. Businesses that are unable to adapt to the intelligence revolution risk being left behind. It's time to reconsider how we all do business.

Identifying Data Trends Before Beginning Your Restart

Every organisation is different, and your AI priorities may differ significantly from those of your competitors. Begin by looking at your data to see if you can spot trends, and then use that knowledge to determine where AI can truly add value to your business.

You can collect massive amounts of data on your customers' habits and preferences, such as how frequently they use your products and services when they use them, and so on. Use your data to create a detailed picture of your customers' behaviours before rethinking your products, services, and processes.

There are three common ways to apply artificial intelligence – products, services, and processes – but they are divided into two categories. The external perspective entails viewing your business through your customer's eyes and looking for ways to make their lives easier by solving their problems and anticipating their needs.

The second point of view is internal. Today's most successful businesses are not only customer-centric but also employee-centric. Internal processes optimized and powered by AI insight help attract and retain the best talent, while also keeping employees happy and engaged in their work.

Provide Personalised Services

Improved customer insights enable you to deliver more intelligent, highly personalised services. Amazon, for example, uses the data it collects automatically from its consumers to create one of the most successful product suggestion engines in the world. The same can be said about Netflix's video-on-demand service.

Netflix's AI doesn't simply provide broad movie or TV program recommendations; it makes highly personalised recommendations based on the time of day you watch, the actors you like, and other viewing habits.

If you've seen several films in which Robert De Niro appears, Netflix can recommend another De Niro film – even one in which he has a minor role. If De Niro isn't in the movie preview image that Netflix usually uses, the AI can pique your interest with a different image that does. That personalised image will make the movie more appealing to you and increase the likelihood that you will continue watching.

Netflix's goal is to put the right movie in front of you at the right time. How can your organisation tailor its services so that they present the best options to your customers at the precise moment they are required?

Smart Product Expansion on a Massive Scale

Because of the Internet of Things, many everyday products are becoming smarter. We can now incorporate increased computing power and small, less expensive sensors into products, allowing us to create smart TVs, smartphones, health monitoring devices, and other devices.

I predict that artificial intelligence will be present in almost all products very soon. Seems far-fetched, doesn't it? Consider this: there is already an AI-enabled "smart diaper" that uses a built-in moisture sensor to notify your phone or watch when a nappy needs to be changed.

A smart toothbrush that detects how well you've brushed your teeth is also available. You can check whether any places need to be cleaned more thoroughly using an app on your phone.

These intelligent products not only enhance customers' lives but also offer significant commercial advantages in terms of customer retention, satisfaction, favourable ratings, and higher income.

Using AI to Simplify Your Business Processes

The world's most successful companies are also leveraging artificial intelligence to optimise, streamline, and automate their business processes across the entire supply chain. AI can be used in almost any business function, including human resources, manufacturing, marketing, sales, quality control, information technology, and finance. Begin by identifying which areas are most critical to your business and where AI might possibly offer the greatest value. Don't simply add AI for the sake of having it; instead, think about what your business wants to achieve and how AI might help you get there.

Artificial Intelligence Can Transform Your Business. Organisations can use AI to improve their business results in three ways: by providing smarter services, developing intelligent products, and improving business processes.

ARTIFICIAL INTELLIGENCE'S IMPORTANCE FOR SMALL BUSINESSES

Artificial intelligence is no longer just for large corporations like Amazon and Facebook. Artificial intelligence and machine learning are benefiting small and medium-sized businesses all over the world – and integrating AI into core business functions and processes is becoming more accessible and affordable by the day.

AI Innovation for Small Businesses

Artificial intelligence is now available 'as-a-service', which is a critical change that has enabled smaller businesses to benefit from it. With this change, artificial intelligence (AI) becomes a reality for more businesses because they no longer need to develop their competencies or infrastructure to benefit from AI. Companies do not even have to use their data; they can use data collected by companies such as Microsoft, Amazon, and Google and then turn it into insight. They don't have to build their own AI, which puts artificial intelligence within most organisations' budgets.

AI-enabled services are another way AI is making its way into smaller organisations. If you use any of the leading cloud-based accounting, HR, marketing, or CRM tools, you are already using AI. Salesforce, HubSpot, SuccessFactors, and QuickBooks, to name a few, are excellent examples.

Five Examples of How Artificial Intelligence Can Benefit Small Businesses

1. Create a plan for staffing, ordering, and inventory management. A butcher shop could use weather data to forecast sunny days and stock up on burgers and hot dogs for spring and summer barbecues.

2.   Recognise trends. SMEs can check for increases in search traffic for keywords using Google trends. This can assist them in planning and developing successful products and services.

3.   Create, automate, and personalise marketing campaigns. AI email algorithms can assist businesses in creating automated messages that are triggered by subscriber activity. AI is built into many CMS and email service platforms, and you can use it right away.

4.   Simplify time-consuming HR tasks. Businesses can use AI to match candidates to open positions, onboard new employees, and answer frequently asked questions about benefits and company policy.

5.   Allow customers to get a firsthand look at products. Small and medium-sized businesses (SMEs) can use augmented reality and artificial intelligence to provide customers with a virtual tour of products in their catalog. Consider a virtual "showroom" of furniture that a customer can customise to meet their specific requirements.

If you're a small or medium-sized business owner who thinks artificial intelligence is a technology you can't utilise or afford, I urge you to rethink!

Small businesses are more relevant to AI than you may believe, and it's essential that you approach AI strategically and use it to boost your company's performance.

CHAPTER TWELVE
THE INTELLIGENT FUTURE OF AI

The most difficult abilities to achieve are those that necessitate interacting with unrestricted and unprepared surroundings. Designing systems with these capabilities necessitates the integration of development in a wide range of AI areas. We particularly require knowledge-representation languages that codify information about a wide range of objects, situations, actions, and so on, as well as their properties and interrelationships—particularly cause-and-effect relationships. We also require new algorithms that can use these representations to solve problems and answer questions on almost any subject robustly and efficiently. Finally, because they will need to learn an almost infinite amount of information, those systems must be able to learn continuously throughout their existence.

To summarise, it is critical to create systems that integrate perception, representation, reasoning, action, and learning. This is a critical AI problem because we still don't know how to integrate all these intelligence components. We require cognitive architectures (Forbus, 2012) that adequately integrate these components. Integrated systems are a critical first step toward achieving general AI someday.

We think that hybrid systems, which combine the benefits of systems capable of reasoning based on knowledge and memory usage (Graves *et al.*, 2016) with those of AI based on large data analysis, *i.e.,* deep learning, will be the most significant study topics in the future (Bengio, 2009). The phenomenon known as "catastrophic forgetting" is presently limiting deep-learning systems. This implies that if they're taught to do one thing (say, play Go) and then taught to do something else (say, differentiate between pictures of dogs and cats), they'll forget all they learned in the prior job (in this case, playing Go).

This limitation is strong evidence that those systems do not learn anything, at least not in humans. Another significant limitation of these systems is that they are "black boxes" with no capability for explanation. It would be fascinating to investigate ways to give deep-learning systems an explicative capability by adding modules that enable them to explain how they arrived at the suggested findings and conclusions, since the ability to explain is an essential feature of any intelligent system. Energy consumption may become one of the most important obstacles to AI development; therefore, new learning algorithms that do not need huge quantities of data to be taught and much more energy-efficient hardware to execute them are needed. In comparison, the brain is orders of magnitude more efficient than the current hardware required to implement the most sophisticated AI algorithms. One avenue to investigate is memristor-based neuromorphic computing.

Humanoid robotics, multimodal person-machine communication, artificial vision, experience-based reasoning, Multiagent systems, action planning, and especially new trends in development robotics may hold the key to giving machines common sense, especially the ability to learn the relationships between their actions and the effects they have on their surroundings.

Significant progress will also be made in biomimetic approaches to replicating animal behaviour in machines. It's not just a matter of reproducing an animal's behaviour; it's also a matter of understanding how the brain that produces that behaviour works. This entails creating and programming electronic circuits that mimic the cerebral activity that is responsible for this behaviour. Some biologists are interested in efforts to build the most complex artificial brain possible because they believe it will help them better understand that organ. Engineers in this context are looking for biological information that will help them create more efficient designs. Molecular biology and recent advances in optogenetics will allow researchers to determine which genes and neurons are involved in various cognitive activities.

In terms of applications, the Web, video games, personal assistants, and autonomous robots will remain among the most important (especially autonomous vehicles, social robots, robots for planetary exploration, and so on). Environmental and energy-saving applications, as well as those for economics and sociology, will be important. Finally, AI applications for the arts (visual arts, music, dance, narrative) will significantly alter the nature of the creative process.

Computers are no longer just tools for creating; they have evolved into creative agents in their own right. This has resulted in a new and promising AI field known as computational creativity, producing very interesting results in chess, music, the visual arts, and narrative, among other creative activities.

PREDICTIONS FOR ARTIFICIAL INTELLIGENCE: HOW MACHINE LEARNING WILL CHANGE EVERYTHING

Throughout the last decade, it was difficult to avoid predictions that artificial intelligence was about to change the world. In the foreseeable future, this is unlikely to alter. On the other side, a greater focus on repeatable and measurable outcomes is likely to anchor some "big picture" ideas in reality.

Don't get me wrong: AI and machine learning will continue to make headlines in the future, and there will likely be more sensationalised claims about robots attempting to take our jobs or even destroying us. Stories about true innovation and progress, on the other hand, should gain prominence as the promise of smart, learning machines begins to bear fruit.

Here are some predictions for what we can expect soon.

AI will have less hype and hot air – but a lot more action

Any new technology generates a lot of buzz. Because the arrival of functional and useful AI has been predicted for centuries, it's not surprising that people want to talk about it now that it's here.

It also implies that there will inevitably be a lot of hot air – for starters, check out my list of the most common AI myths. This will inevitably fade as the media shifts to the "next big thing." In time, I believe we will begin to see real progress toward achieving some of the dreams and ambitions that have been discussed in recent years.

All indicators indicate that investment in the development and integration of AI, particularly machine learning, technology is increasing in scale. Furthermore, results are beginning to emerge that go beyond computers learning to beat humans at board games and TV game shows. I expect a continuous stream of small but important leaps ahead soon as machine learning and neural network technologies take on more routine tasks. Once new techniques are mastered, they propagate very quickly.

More money than ever before will be poured into AI enterprise projects

As a result of the successes of innovators and market leaders, an increasing number of their businesses will launch AI-related initiatives.

With self-driving cars and ships on the horizon, as well as life-saving medical advances, it appears likely that the pace of technological change will accelerate as the decade comes to a close. Acting on the newly available potential for change is becoming an increasingly urgent priority for many CEOs and CTOs.

The fear of missing out (FOMO) is another powerful motivator. With so much to gain, a mindset of "we have to do something" with AI may emerge. While this could serve as a motivator, if action is taken too quickly, it could easily lead to my next prediction:

Many AI projects will fail at a high cost

This is a sad fact about many projects that involve new and often untested technology that has existed throughout history. In some cases, it comes down to the risks that each pioneer is willing to take. The only certainty when working on a new frontier is that there will be unexpected difficulties. Although machine learning algorithms are excellent at devising new solutions to problems and appear to be capable of forecasting the future, they are unlikely to anticipate or respond to many of the internal and external factors that could influence success. These may include management and workforce buy-in, legal, political, or economic developments, competitor activities, and the ability of business and data-centric teams to collaborate.

A lack of clarity or focus on the goals and expectations of an AI initiative is frequently a cause of failure. Even Behemoths such as IBM have recently had massive failures, such as 'Watson' for healthcare, losing billions of investment. The harsh reality is that AI is difficult and frequently costly. A trend toward "plug and play" as-a-service solutions may have prompted organisations with less than global-scale resources to consider incorporating AI. However, it risks encouraging a "one-size-fits-all" or templated approach to data science, which may not be appropriate for the goals of every organisation.

The initiatives and projects that are most likely to succeed are planned from the start with a clear strategy and results that are clearly tied to bottom-line KPIs like revenue growth and customer satisfaction scores.

There will be more technological interaction with humans

We will continue to interact with machines through voice. Conversational interfaces, like how Echo and Alexa have infiltrated our homes, will become more prevalent when it comes to engaging with technology in the workplace.

According to one report, 20% of businesses will look to add voice-enabled interfaces to their existing point-and-click dashboards and systems next year. After all, it's the most natural method for most of us to communicate - we can usually formulate any question in seconds. As computers' ability to understand humans has improved, we no longer need to spend time mastering their complicated mathematical languages. Natural language generation and processing algorithms are continuously increasing their capacity to understand us and communicate with us in a manner that we can comprehend. This will continue to develop, and we should eventually be able to converse with robots within specific limits, just as we would with another human.

Robots will be more closely involved in our health and well-being

Okay, so the prediction is a little dramatic, but I'm not saying we'll walk into the doctor's office and be greeted by a robotic humanoid (at least not yet). Artificial intelligence is infiltrating healthcare in a way that will initially be invisible to patients. Image recognition algorithms are being used behind the scenes to detect warning signs buried in medical images and even handwritten doctors' notes. Because this technology has proven to be successful in pilots, we expect it to be in wider operational use within the next year. More robots with the ability to assist people with disabilities and illnesses are also likely to appear in people's homes. Care and companionship robots are expected to gain popularity and may one day become commonplace.

CONCLUSION

No matter how rapidly future artificial intelligence progresses, it is on a trajectory to eclipse human intelligence, even if requires multiple systems to be integrated into a 'singularity' to become 'general intelligence'. As previously stated, the mental development required for all complex intelligence is dependent on interactions with the environment, and those interactions, in turn, are dependent on the body—particularly the perceptive and motor systems. This, combined with the fact that machines will go through parallel socialisation and culture-acquisition processes as humans, reinforces the conclusion that these intelligences, no matter how sophisticated they become, will be distinct from ours but significantly more efficient.

The existence of intelligence, unlike ours, and thus alien to our values and human needs, necessitates consideration of the potential ethical limitations of AI development. We specifically agree with Weizenbaum's assertion (Weizenbaum, 1976) that no machine should ever make entirely autonomous decisions or provide advice that requires, among other things, wisdom derived from human experiences and recognition of human values.

The true threat of AI is not the highly improbable technological singularity produced by the existence of hypothetical future artificial superintelligences; the true threats are already present. Today's algorithms powering Internet search engines or recommendation and personal-assistant systems on our cellphones already have a good understanding of what we do, our preferences, and tastes. They can even deduce what we are thinking and how we are feeling.

Access to massive amounts of data that we willingly produce is essential for this since evaluating data from different sources shows connections and patterns that would be impossible to discover without AI methods. Therefore, an alarming loss of privacy has occurred. To prevent this, we should have the right to own a copy of any personal data we produce, to govern its use, and to determine who has access to it and under what circumstances, rather than entrusting it to big companies that have no clue what they're doing with it. This is quite practical with today's technologies, just not in the interests of service providers with their current business models.

AI is based on complex programming, which means that mistakes are unavoidable. Even if it were possible to create completely dependable software, there are ethical quandaries that software developers must consider when designing it. For example, an autonomous vehicle may decide to run over a pedestrian to avoid a collision that would be dangerous to its occupants. Equipping businesses with advanced AI systems that improve management and production efficiency will necessitate fewer human employees, resulting in increased unemployment. Many AI experts are emphasising the importance of regulating AI development because of these ethical quandaries, suggesting its use should be prohibited in some cases, citing the example of self-driving cars.

Proportionality (avoiding disproportionate use of force), discrimination (the need to distinguish between combatants and civilians, or between a combatant surrendering and one preparing to attack), and precaution (minimising the number of victims and material damage) are extremely difficult to assess, making it nearly impossible for AI systems in autonomous weapons to follow them. Even if machines were to achieve this capability in the very long term, it would be 'impolite' to delegate the decision to kill to a machine.

Aside from this type of regulation, it is critical to educate the public about the dangers of intelligent technologies and to ensure that they have the necessary skills to control them rather than being controlled by them. Our future citizens must be much more informed, with a greater ability to assess technological risks, a stronger critical sense, and a willingness to exercise their rights. This training must begin in school and continue through university. It is especially important for science and engineering students to receive ethics training so that they can better understand the social implications of the technologies they will almost certainly develop. Only by investing in education will we be able to create a society that can reap the benefits of intelligent technology while minimising the risks. AI has undeniably enormous potential to benefit society if we use it correctly and prudently. It is necessary to raise awareness of AI's limitations and to act collectively to ensure that AI is used for the common good in a safe, dependable, and responsible manner.

The path to truly intelligent AI will remain long and difficult. After all, this field is only sixty years old, and, as Carl Sagan would have pointed out, sixty years is a mere blink of an eye on a cosmic time scale. In his 1936 speech "The Cataclysm of Damocles," Gabriel Garcia Márquez put it more poetically: "It took 380 million years for a butterfly to learn to fly, 180 million years for a rose to be created with no other commitment than to be beautiful, and four geological periods for us humans to be able to sing better than birds and die from love since the emergence of visible life on Earth."

ABOUT THE AUTHOR

Safa Al Ameri

Chief Innovation Officer and Multi award winning and yet humble in outlook, Safa has completed the MSc in Artificial Intelligence as well as an MBA, with distinction - she is perfectly placed to help encourage and support other students during the early stages of their studies.

With clear decision making, coming from years of examinations experience at Department of Health in Abu Dhabi, UAE. Her passion is to make AI explainable to those who use it - especially in healthcare so we can all benefit from this major advance in technology.

AI Insights

The AI Insights Series is both a reflection of the personal experience of authors as they come to live with AI, and the essence of understanding how we can augment our own intelligence by using such tools. The series deep dives into specific areas with experts in each domain. The books are intended to be both easily read and portable so they may be carried with you to fill those gaps in the day.

As part of a community of AI specialists, we believe strongly in "explainable" AI, to demystify and help people with the awareness of how such tools will be part of our everyday lives.
 Artificial Intelligence Story & History - The primer to the AI Insights series, this book helps the novice navigate the ways in which AI is changing our lives, exploring questions, and providing straightforward explanations in human readable terms.

AI is here to stay - it leads the way for humanity in many avenues shining new light by taking raw data and creating new models and theories to guide us, based on sound evidence. Explainable AI Explainable AI principles are that the system should be able to explain its output and provide supporting evidence (at least), so the given explanation must be meaningful, enabling users to complete their tasks. This explanation needs to be clear and accurate, which is different from output accuracy. This book therefore focuses on how to make this happen.

Personal AI In the near future, we will apply our responsible AI principles with guidance - Learning how responsible AI governance is crucial to guiding AI innovation not just on a corporate scale but reflecting your own personal activities and your own private networks. This book outlines how we will take control of our own AI environments and foster collaboration between AI systems.